P9-CEE-539

FINISH THIS BOOK

KERI SMITH

PENGUIN BOOKS

PENGUIN BOOKS
An imprint of Penguin Random House LLC
375 Hudson Street
New York, New York 10014
penguin.com

First published in the United States of America by Perigee, an imprint of Penguin Group (USA) Inc., 2011
Published in Penguin Books 2016

ISBN: 978-0-399-53689-2

Printed in the United States of America

20

This book is dedicated to all explorers and future explorers of the world.

He pushes his eyeglasses up on his brow. "Yes, a novel that begins like that..." he says, "I could swear I've read it... You have only this beginning and would like to find the continuation, is that true? The trouble is that once upon a time they all began like that, all novels. There was somebody who went along a lonely street and saw something that attracted his attention, something that seemed to conceal a mystery, or a premonition; then he asked for explanations and they told him a long story..."

–Italo Calvino, If on a Winter's Night a Traveler

INSTRUCTIONS

1. COMPLETE THIS BOOK IN ORDER. DO NOT SKIP AHEAD (UNLESS INSTRUCTED TO). YOU WILL BE PRESENTED WITH ASSIGNMENTS AS YOU NEED TO LEARN THEM.

2. DO NOT SHARE YOUR FINDINGS UNTIL DIRECTED TO DO SO.

3. IF AT ANY TIME YOU FIND YOURSELF UNABLE TO COMPLETE THE TASKS IN THE BOOK, PLEASE FORWARD THE BOOK TO SOMEONE YOU FEEL WILL BE ABLE TO COMPLETE IT.

START HERE

Somehow this book has ended up in your hands. Maybe you picked it up while browsing in the store after becoming bored by the other books and something about it called out to you. Or perhaps you got it as a gift. Whatever the case, the very premise intrigues you. Of course it's ridiculous to purchase a book that is not finished (why would someone publish an unfinished book in the first place?), but there is a part of you that feels maybe this is "your" book—the book you were meant to complete. You realize you have to take it home.

Mark the location where you found this book on the map below. (If this map is not accurate, feel free to correct it.)

NAME Mia Venditte DATE 12/25/20

ADDRESS 12 buccaneer bend + 5091 highbridge street

CITY Syracuse ZIP 13066 PHONE 315-450-5018

NOTES
DATE OF BIRTH: 5/30/07
PLACE OF BIRTH: St Joe's hospital
ALIAS: Mimi
LIKES: pasta, Christmas, tik tok, strawberry
DISLIKES: Cheese, baked beans, donald trump
DREAMS: being a teacher or social worker
NOTES ABOUT HOW YOU CAME IN CONTACT WITH FINISH THIS BOOK: For 2020 Xmas Eve, My Aunt Gabby gifted me this book

PLACE YOUR FINGERPRINTS HERE (USE DIRT IF YOU DON'T HAVE ANY INK):

SIT DOWN

Sit down with this book and start reading.

Wait! Stop! Before you start, you should make a sign to hang nearby, and it should say something like, "Do not disturb! I am finishing my book! Signed, [your name]." Cut it out and hang it. Now you can start.

Do NOT disturb! I am finishing my book!

Signed, Mia

(You can use a blank sheet of paper if you don't want to cut this page.)

BEGIN

Now that you know you won't be disturbed, you may feel a bit hesitant to begin—the blank pages seem too pristine, too crisp, and you worry about "messing them up." Or maybe you feel like you can't wait to get started.

Either way, don't worry about all of the voices in your head. Instead, search for your favorite pen, the one you enjoy writing with the most these days. Is it in your bag? Your desk?

Once you've found it, change into your comfiest clothes and make a cup of your favorite drink.* Sit down with your drink and pen.

And begin.

Two Methods to Find a Favorite Pen If You Do Not Have One

Method #1. Consider all of the qualities you find beneficial/pleasing in a writing utensil and make a list (for example, writes smoothly, black ink, feels good in the hand). Go on a quest to find a pen that satisfies all of the items on your list. (This could take years.)

Method #2. Find a pen that writes. Do not worry too much about its qualities. Enact a small ceremony to imbue it with special powers. (Some ideas: decorate it, assign it a special name, anoint it with a "magic substance" like fairy dust, etc.)

*Some drink suggestions include tea, hot chocolate, coffee, a smoothie, or a milkshake.

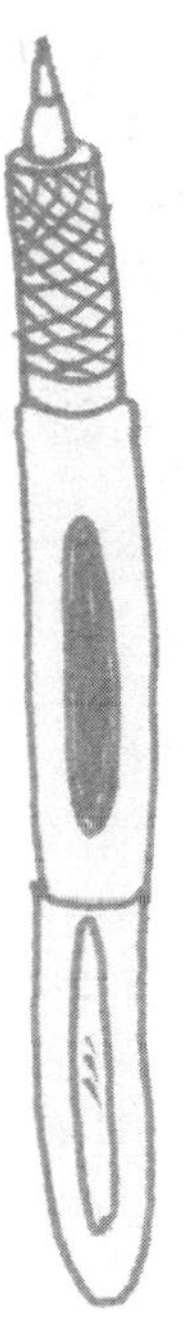

This is my favorite Pen

(Test your favorite pen here.)

MAKE A DECISION

Now I would like to share with you the reason for this book's existence. But be warned: once you read the following pages, you will not be able to return to your previous life of not finishing unfinished books, and you may wish that you had never purchased this ridiculous book in the first place. But don't worry—you have a chance to back out. In fact, right now, you can close this book, place it among the other books on your bookshelf, or give it away, and never think about it ever again.

So, make a decision:

1. Close the book. Hide it on a shelf, or give it to a friend who you think would like it. (Someone who's into mysteries, perhaps?)

OR

2. Continue to the next page and find out why this book exists.

GATHER SOME TOOLS

You are still here. Well, then, it is best to read on as you have demonstrated that you are the person to finish this book . . . the one I have been waiting for.

Before we proceed, there are some tools you must acquire. You are going to need them to complete the tasks in this book.

You must have:

A journal
A pair of scissors
Some glue
A stapler
A needle and thread (optional)
A digital camera (optional)
A good eye
A courageous spirit

Collect these items and place them next to you. You may wish to take a photo of them for documentation purposes.*

*And to leave a trail for others in case you are unable to complete your task.

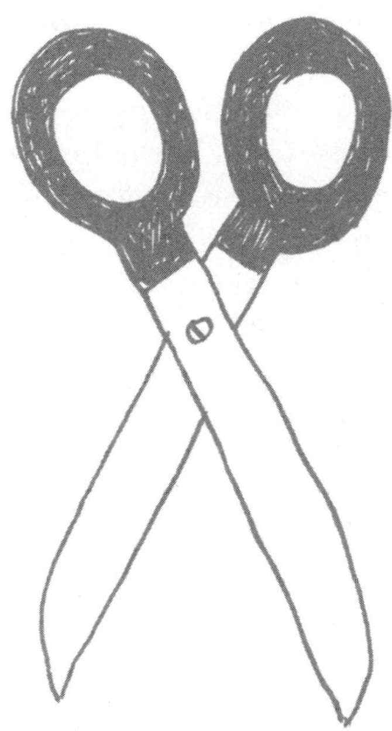

THE STORY

It is time to explain how this book came to be and the reason it exists—the mysterious secret, the reason you are here . . .

Several years ago, I was on my way home after spending a long day in the library doing research. In the last few years, I had become obsessed with making connections between various books and ideas, and began spending large amounts of time investigating all manner of things. I had started to see the world as an intensely fascinating and seemingly unlimited place, full of an almost infinite number of books, many with wonderfully enticing titles. On this day, I had spent a few hours reading The Library of Babel* and covertly sipping green tea until the sun went down.

Suddenly, I realized the time and that I was at risk of missing dinner entirely, so I packed up my things and ran out of the room, leaving the book I had been reading spinning wildly on the desk. (You can re-create this effect using this book right now if you'd like. Close it up first. It's rather fun to try.)

Outside, the night was warm for the time of year, which was fall, and there were leaves blowing wildly all around. It was threatening to rain and little flashes of lightning were flickering in the distance. I would have to hurry so as not to get caught in the impending storm.

To get to my house, I passed through a park, which had a long and windy path. Every 20 feet or so there was a park bench, of the standard wood and cast-iron variety. (Please draw one on the opposite page.)

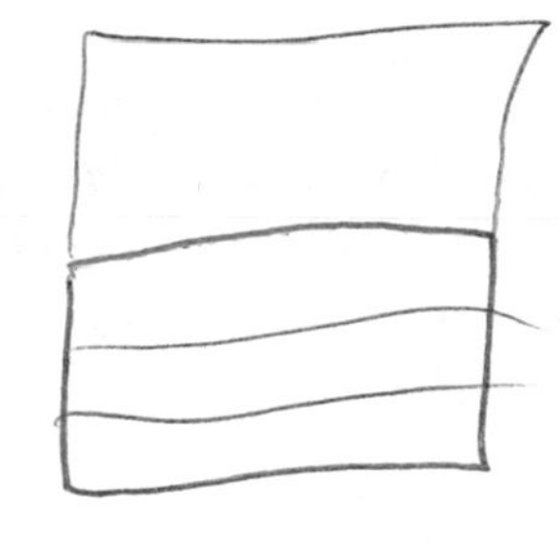

(Draw park bench here.)

THE STORY PT 2

Though my head was filled with images from the book I had been reading, I noticed that one of the benches had a bunch of papers scattered haphazardly around it. Not being the kind of person who can just walk by random papers I find on the street, I went over to the bench and began to read, first looking around to see if anyone was watching. I confirmed I was alone.

The first page with text that I found looked like this:

I thought maybe it was some kind of strange code. I began to gather up all of the other pages. Even though it was windy, there was a fence right behind the bench that, luckily, served to catch the scattered pages, so collecting them proved much easier than I'd expected. I grabbed what looked to be a worn black cardboard cover and quickly shoved the loose sheets into my book bag, right next to my dog-eared copy of Calvino's If on a Winter's Night a Traveler. I ran the rest of the way home. Just as I reached the front step of my house, it started to rain.

Once inside I threw off my coat and pulled out the pages I'd found. There seemed to be no coherent order, or none that I could identify at first glance. The cover appeared to be blank, but on closer inspection I realized there was a largish mud smear that had obscured the title. I rubbed it off with my finger and one by one the letters appeared:

INSTRUCTION MANUAL

And so began the mystery. Who created the Instruction Manual and what was its purpose? I quickly became determined to find out. However, for reasons I do not wish to get into at this time, I'm now passing the task on, which is why you are here staring intently at these very pages.

A facsimile of the manual has been re-created for you later in this book. But don't turn to it yet; there are still a few things we need to address.

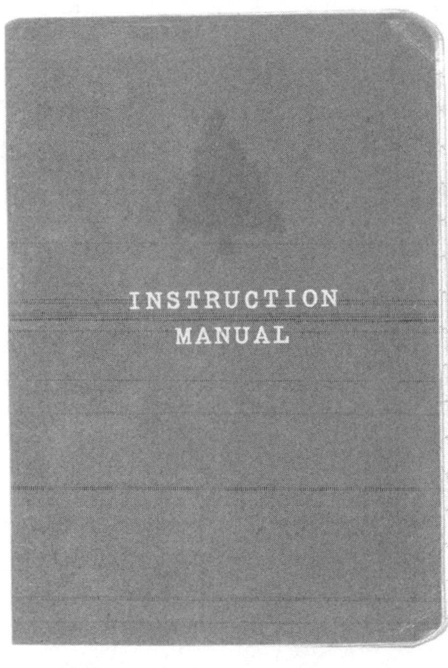
INSTRUCTION
MANUAL

BECOMING A SLEUTH

You may be feeling slightly overwhelmed by the fact that the outcome of this book depends on you. This is a much bigger job than you thought. Don't worry; we will begin slowly and get you started with some secret intelligence techniques, as well as documentation and observation methods commonly employed by sleuths. Sleuths are required to notice, observe, and make sense of the world around them—all traits that will help you solve the mystery of this book.

Research: definition of "sleuthing"
Research methods: dictionary, Internet, library

SECRET INTELLIGENCE TRAINING

OPERATION: INSTRUCTION MANUAL

SECRET INTELLIGENCE TRAINING

OPERATION: WARM-UP

STATUS: ☐ IN PROGRESS ☐ COMPLETED

First, a warm-up exercise.

Think of an interesting way to fill in this page. Use this as an opportunity to try something you've never tried before. A good sleuth is always willing to try something new.

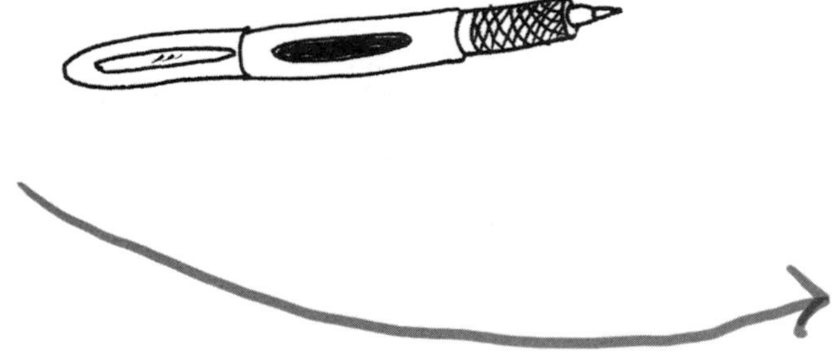

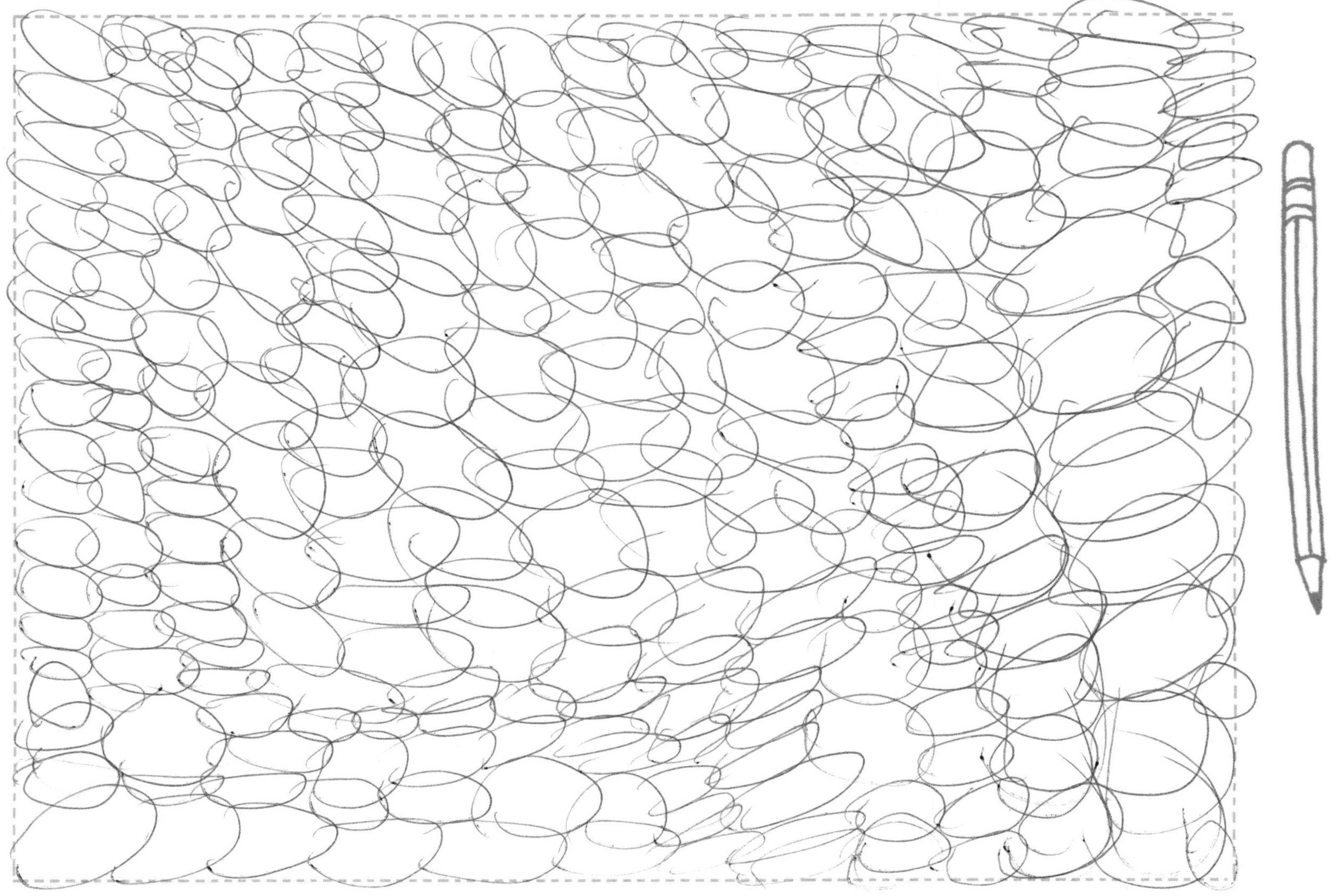

SECRET INTELLIGENCE TRAINING

OPERATION: DRESS-UP

STATUS: ☐ IN PROGRESS ☐ COMPLETED

Now that you've gotten warmed up, we are going to do some more intensive exercises. The following pages will help develop your innate skills. DO NOT SKIP OVER THESE STEPS. Doing so may result in a failure to finish this book.

We must first test your ability to go undercover, in case you are required to hide your identity.

INSTRUCTIONS

1. Cut out the disguise to the left. (If you don't wish to cut out this page, this disguise is repeated in the back of this book on the template page.)
2. Affix it to your face using whatever method necessary.
3. Take a photo of yourself in disguise.
4. Paste it here.

SECRET INTELLIGENCE TRAINING

OPERATION: CODE CRACKING 1

STATUS: ☐ IN PROGRESS ☐ COMPLETED

A few codes you might like to try:

SUBSTITUTION CIPHER WHEEL

Cut out the two wheels (the Decoder is also repeated in the back of this book on the template page). Place the smaller wheel on top of the larger wheel. In order to read the code you will need a "key letter," a letter that tells you how to set the wheel, for example, A=G. Rotate the wheels so your key letter on the small wheel is beneath the A of the large wheel. In the case of A=G, you will turn the small wheel so that the G lines up with the A on the large wheel and decipher the code accordingly. So if A=G, then B=H, and so on.

Coded message: Skkz sk gz znk ykixkz ruigzout rgzkx.
Decoded message: Meet me at the secret location later.

DIAGRAMMATIC CIPHER

The diagrammatic cipher substitutes symbols for letters. It uses tic-tac-toe boards and two X's as shown to the right.

Here is the same secret message as above, using the line shapes that surround each letter (and including a dot where needed):

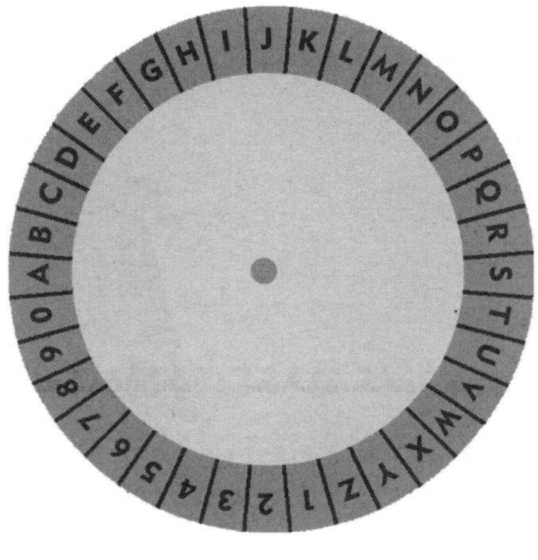
A B C D E F G H I J K L M N O P Q R S T U V W X Y Z 1 2 3 4 5 6 7 8 9 0

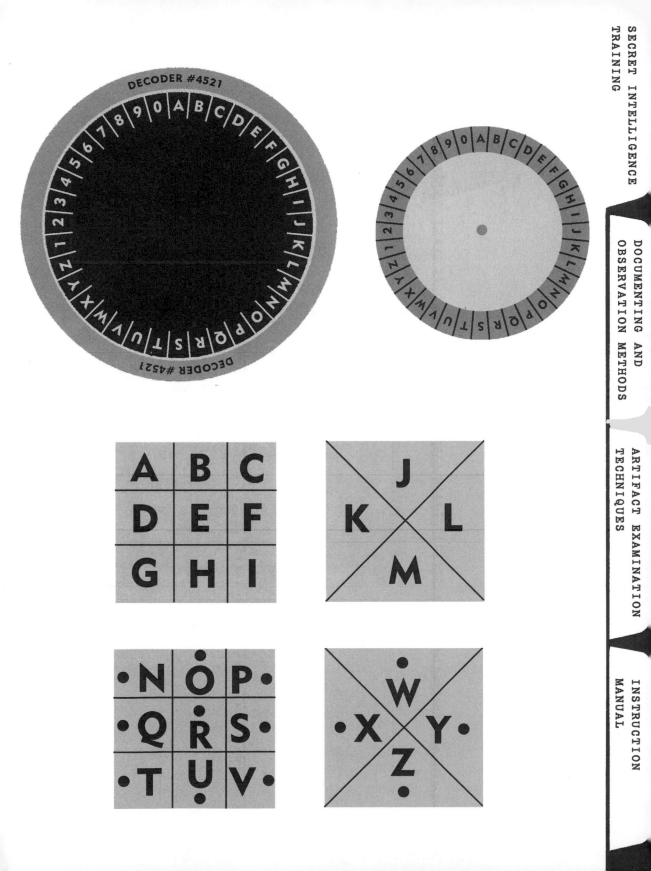

DECODER #4521
A B C D E F G H I J K L M N O P Q R S T U V W X Y Z 1 2 3 4 5 6 7 8 9 0
DECODER #4521

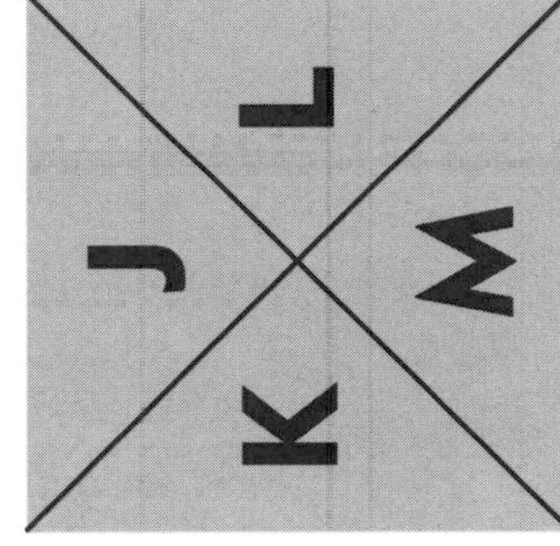
J
K
L
M

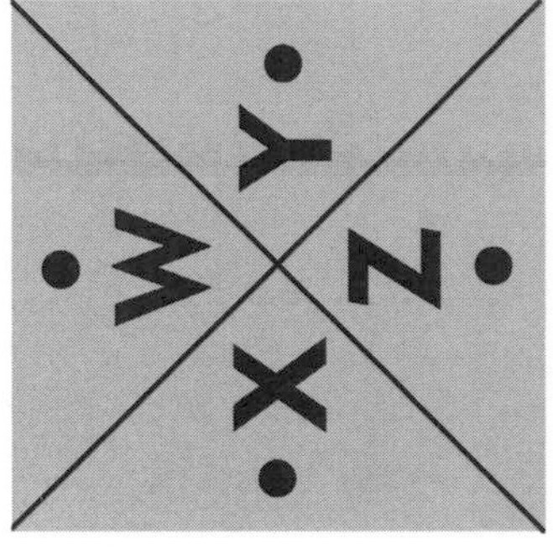
W
X
Y
Z

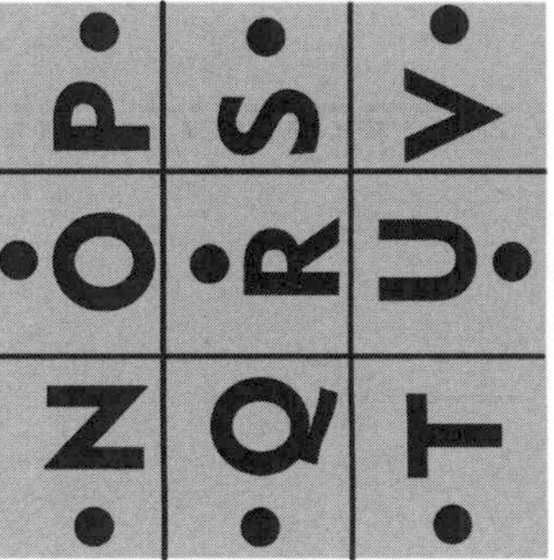
N O P
Q R S
T U V

A B C
D E F
G H I

SECRET INTELLIGENCE TRAINING

OPERATION: CODE CRACKING 2

STATUS: ☐ IN PROGRESS ☐ COMPLETED

TRANSPOSITION CIPHER

With a transposition cipher both the sender and receiver of a code must agree on and remember the method for enciphering and deciphering. In this case, we will use a box shape as it is easy to remember. If you don't have enough characters to make a complete square, you can add a dummy letter or two at the end. (See grid to the left.)

We can now transcribe the message by moving down the columns instead of across the rows. You should break the characters into groups to give no clues about word sizes. The result looks like this:

MAEON ETCCL ETRAA THETT METIE ESLOR

Tip: You may wish to draw a square after the code to help the decoder remember the format you are using.

EXERCISE

Here are some coded messages for you to practice with.

M	E	E	T	M	E
A	T	T	H	E	S
E	C	R	E	T	L
O	C	A	T	I	O
N	L	A	T	E	R

A=R

AYV 76DV9 6W Z4RXZ5RAZ65 4R2V0 BO Z5WZ52ZV.
-16Y5 4BZ9

STHS IHOE MILC PNDR LGTE ESHT ☐

SECRET INTELLIGENCE TRAINING

OPERATION: ATTENTION SKILLS

STATUS: ☐ IN PROGRESS ☐ COMPLETED

The following exercise develops your attention skills so that you can take in information.

Go on a walk in your neighborhood. Look at the ground as you walk. Take notes on how many different colors, shapes, and objects you see. Document them with drawings here.

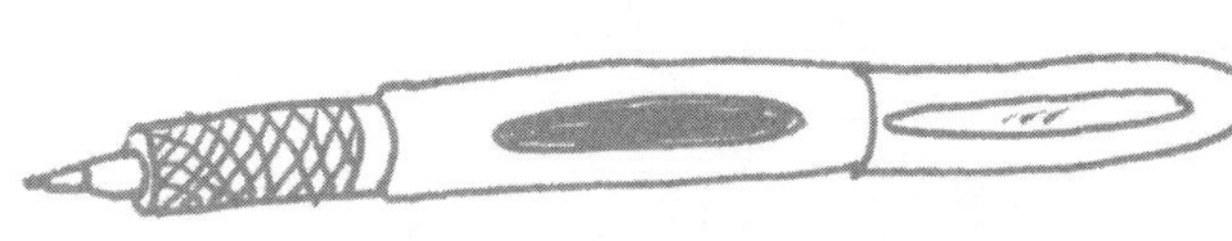

SECRET INTELLIGENCE TRAINING

OPERATION: MEMORY EXERCISE

STATUS: ☐ IN PROGRESS ☐ COMPLETED

Study this photo for a few minutes.
Cover up the image and write down everything you remember from it.

- two small kids
- two men
- one man has glasses
- plants
- in front of house steps

SECRET INTELLIGENCE TRAINING

OPERATION: NEUROBICS

STATUS: ☐ IN PROGRESS ☐ COMPLETED

The following is a series of exercises called neurobics, designed to stimulate your brain for optimal function. Please document your completion of these exercises.

- Perform a series of everyday tasks with your eyes closed. For example, wash your hair, brush your teeth, and get dressed with your eyes closed.

- Share a meal using only visual cues (such as hand gestures) to communicate. No talking.

- Perform a series of everyday tasks with your nondominant hand.

- Break up your routine. Take a completely new route to a place you visit regularly. Try a food you've never tried before. Completely rearrange your room or an area of your house.

Research: neurobics

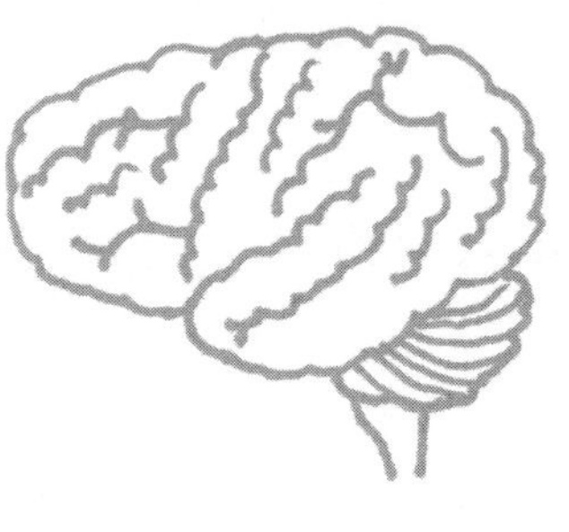

SECRET INTELLIGENCE TRAINING

STATUS: COMPLETE

INSTRUCTIONS: PROCEED TO NEXT SECTION

Congratulations, you have completed the Secret Intelligence Training section and are ready to proceed to Documenting and Observation Methods. Before you proceed, you should have a little mental retreat. Good sleuths always take some necessary downtime to restore their body and mind.

On the next page, create your own little place to retreat to. What do you find restful? It could be an image or a written description. You could create a replica of your favorite spot. Or maybe it is nothing but blank space.

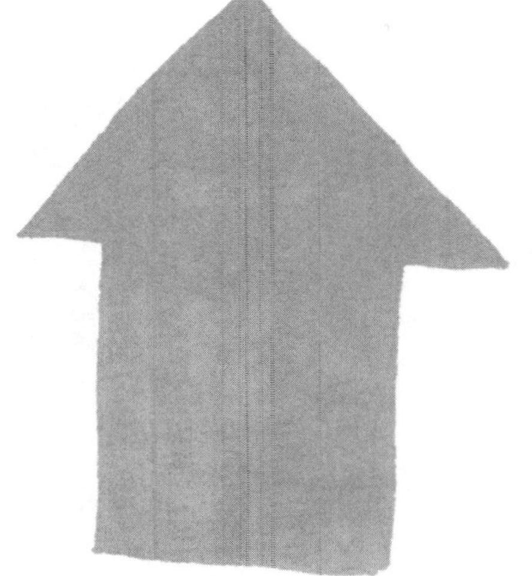

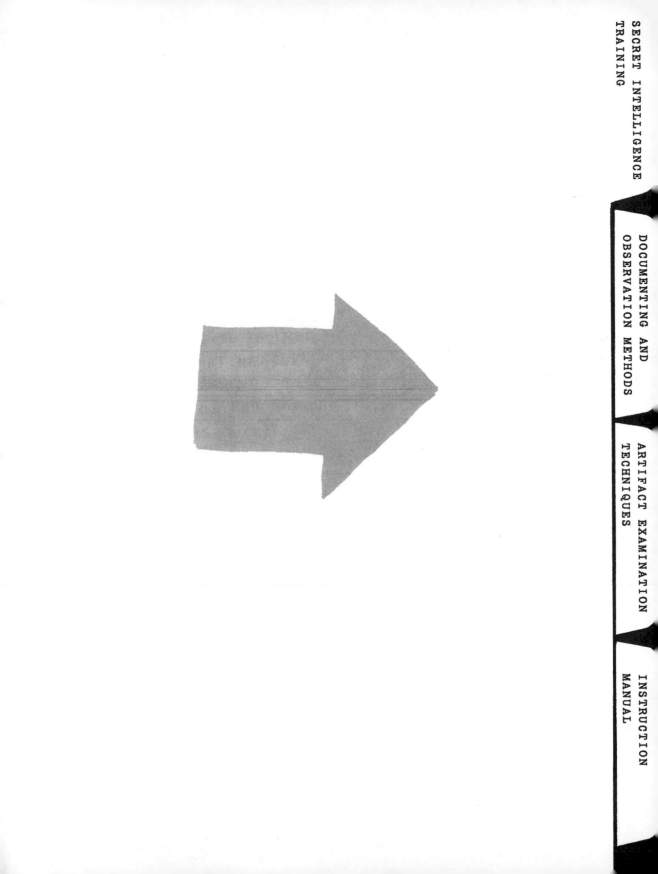

THIS SPACE RESERVED FOR RETREAT SPACE.

DOCUMENTING AND OBSERVATION METHODS

OPERATION: DOCUMENT YOUR DAY

STATUS: ☐ IN PROGRESS ☐ COMPLETED

Now you are ready to get back to business. We will start with the simplest but also most important method: documenting your day. This is necessary so that you become more aware of your daily movement and progress. You can make the entries brief. If you like you can also do some quick sketches.

FIELD NOTES

Date: 12/24/20

8:00 am- Was not awake

9:00 am- Was not awake

10:00 am- Was not awake

11:00 am- Woke up

12:00 pm- took shower

1:00 pm- watched home alone 2 with dad

2:00 pm- folded clothes

3:00 pm- watched gossip girl

4:00 pm- watched Star wars with jay

5:00 pm- dad drove us to nanas

6:00 pm- at nanas house

7:00 pm- ate Xmas eve dinner at nanas

8:00 pm- drove back to moms house

9:00 pm- got my presents together

10:00 pm- Went on social media

11:00 pm- ~~[illegible]~~ hung out with Mom and Amanda, trey, jay, jr in living room

DOCUMENTING AND OBSERVATION METHODS

ARTIFACT EXAMINATION TECHNIQUES

INSTRUCTION MANUAL

DOCUMENTING AND OBSERVATION METHODS

OPERATION: EVIDENCE EXAMINATION

STATUS: ☐ IN PROGRESS ☐ COMPLETED

While involved in any sleuthing endeavor, you will need to examine all surrounding evidence.

Several feet away from where the Instruction Manual was found, there was a subscription card (see reproduction on the right-hand page). The card was sitting in a rather muddy-looking puddle, but it appears to be some kind of advertisement for a publisher.

Study the card in detail. It may remind you of other cards you have seen in magazines, the ones that annoyingly fall to the floor while you are trying to find a certain article that piqued your interest.

Record your observations here:

Postage must be paid by sender.

A=E

BUSINESS REPLY CARD

The Lost Forest Publishing Company

P. O. Box 42-A G. P. O.
Troy, New York 12180

Dear Reader,

The code below will give you access to other titles on our list.

Code: AAA.PJTYFPMWLMRKGS.GSQ

NAME: ______________________

ADDRESS: ______________________

____

DOCUMENTING AND OBSERVATION METHODS

OPERATION: SLEUTH RESEARCH

STATUS: ☐ IN PROGRESS ☐ COMPLETED

You have been engaged in solving the mystery of this book for a while now, and as happens with these things, you are probably developing a relationship with the book, a bonding of sorts. Are you enjoying the life of a sleuth?

Research: famous sleuths. Make a list of at least 10 fictional characters who solve crimes. (If you have a bit of time it would be extremely helpful to read about their techniques.)

DOCUMENTING AND OBSERVATION METHODS

OPERATION: STREAM OF CONSCIOUSNESS

STATUS: ☐ IN PROGRESS ☐ COMPLETED

Listen to your own voice. Good sleuths need to trust their instincts. What is that voice, you ask? It's the one that you listen to every day, and it has a lot of interesting ideas and thoughts and theories, all of which are perfect for recording here. Write your stream of consciousness for several minutes without stopping. Record whatever pops into your head.

DOCUMENTING AND OBSERVATION METHODS

OPERATION: BLIND CONTOUR DRAWING

STATUS: ☐ IN PROGRESS ☐ COMPLETED

Writing about things is one way to research and document. But it is also helpful to draw things in your investigations.

We're going to conduct a quick little experiment now to help loosen you up a bit. It's okay if you think it's silly. What's important is that you try it. A good sleuth is willing to try things even though he or she finds them questionable. That is how they develop the ability to work under a variety of circumstances.

1. Find an object to draw in your immediate environment (simple is good).
2. Grab a pen or whatever you want to draw with.
3. Start with the outermost edge of the object and begin drawing the object. But do NOT look at your drawing!!!
4. Continue to follow the outside edge without looking until you complete the object.

Research: blind contour drawing

(Blind contour drawing)

DOCUMENTING AND OBSERVATION METHODS

OPERATION: COLLECTING

STATUS: ☐ IN PROGRESS ☐ COMPLETED

Another documentation method we can employ is collecting. In your immediate environment collect a variety of objects that you can affix to this page.

Using packing tape or a stapler, attach them here. Write notes beside them about where you found them.

Research: definition of "naturalist"

DOCUMENTING AND OBSERVATION METHODS

OPERATION: POWERS OF OBSERVATION

STATUS: ☐ IN PROGRESS ☐ COMPLETED

Now we will work on your powers of observation. Look at the photo on the left. Write down as many observations as you can. Don't think about it too much. Starting now.

DOCUMENTING AND OBSERVATION METHODS

OPERATION: PORTABLE SLEUTHING KIT

STATUS: ☐ IN PROGRESS ☐ COMPLETED

We're almost ready to go out into the world. But before you can do that, you'll need to put together your very own Portable Sleuthing Kit, which will allow you to conduct research in a variety of ways.

Please assemble the following items and draw them here:

decoder wheel
code breaker
flashlight
magnifying glass
pen
ruler
ink pad
fingerprint template
notebook (for taking notes, writing down clues, etc.)
water (it's important to stay hydrated)
compass
chalk
a container for everything (pencil case, bag, etc.)

Now that your Portable Sleuthing Kit is complete you are ready to go outside to conduct your research.

(Portable Sleuthing Kit)

DOCUMENTING AND OBSERVATION METHODS

OPERATION: MAPPING

STATUS: ☐ IN PROGRESS ☐ COMPLETED

Take a walk around your neighborhood just to get your thoughts flowing more freely. Attempt to locate some kind of snack to eat on your travels. Find a nice place to sit. As you have now officially begun this secret mission, it would be helpful if you documented your movements.

Draw a map of your neighborhood, and mark the spot where you are currently sitting. Include a brief description of the place. (This will be important for reference purposes, and in case you fail on your mission and others must follow your path.)

Look around you. There is always a lot to see even in the most boring of circumstances. Look closer.

(Map of your neighborhood.)

DOCUMENTING AND OBSERVATION METHODS

OPERATION: INFRAORDINARY

STATUS: ☐ IN PROGRESS ☐ COMPLETED

How many things in the world do you pass on an average day, and yet don't take in? How often do you notice the moon during the day? It is often there. What about the color of the sky? Do you notice it now? The texture of whatever you are sitting on? The number of different smells?

Write a list of other things that you notice now (but did not before): colors, shapes, textures, smells, etc.

Research: infraordinary

DOCUMENTING AND OBSERVATION METHODS

OPERATION: HOME BASE

STATUS: ☐ IN PROGRESS ☐ COMPLETED

Time to go back to your house or office or special place, which we will now refer to as home base. When you arrive, make a quick map of it. In this case an overhead view will work best, so others get an idea of the layout.

Can you find a secret location in your home base to hide this book? Mark it on the map.

Research: cartography

(Map of home base.)

DOCUMENTING AND OBSERVATION METHODS

OPERATION: OBJECT DOCUMENTATION

STATUS: ☐ IN PROGRESS ☐ COMPLETED

After looking around home base, think about some of the objects you have collected over the years. What things are most important to you? Which is your favorite?

Document as many things about your favorite object as you can in list form.

Write a short history of your favorite object (as of right now).

Research: ethnography

DOCUMENTING AND OBSERVATION METHODS

OPERATION: CONNECTION-MAKING/DIVINATION

STATUS: ☐ IN PROGRESS ☐ COMPLETED

There are schools of thought that believe all experiences are connected in some way. A good sleuth is able to search out these connections in the world. One exercise that helps illustrate connections is a form of divination called bibliomancy.

METHOD

1. Pick a book. Don't search around for the coolest book you can find. Choose what's actually closest to you.
2. Balance it on its spine and allow it to fall open.
3. With your eyes closed, pick a passage.
4. Write the passage here.

How does this passage connect to your life? With very little effort everything can be shown to connect with everything else.

Research: bibliomancy

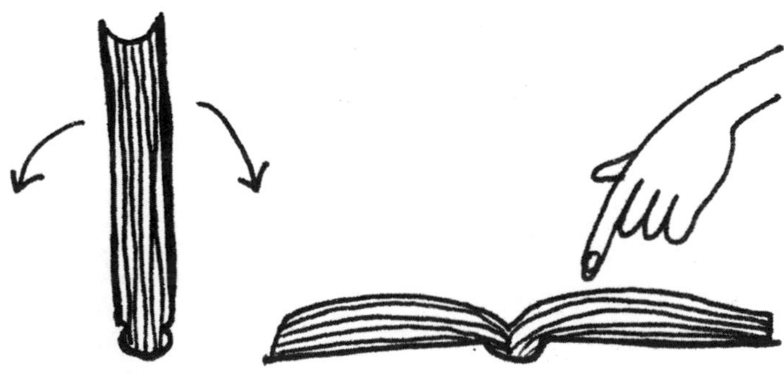

DOCUMENTING AND OBSERVATION METHODS

OPERATION: QUESTIONING REALITY

STATUS: ☐ IN PROGRESS ☐ COMPLETED

Sometimes, a sleuth needs to think beyond the usual structure and routine. What is structure anyway? Is it not just a formula created by others? A set of rules based on someone else's beliefs of what you should be doing?*

Who says we must do what others have done? Is it not important to veer off course now and then? To do something completely unpredictable?

For a moment, forget the rules this book has shared so far . . . forget even that you're holding a book. What if this object had a life outside these pages? What might that look like? What if this page moved around?

Find a way to give this page a new life.

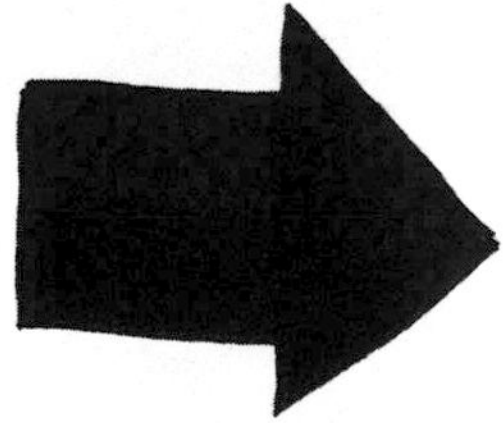

*Consider this: Everything you have been taught about the world may or may not be true.

Research: definition of "literary structure"

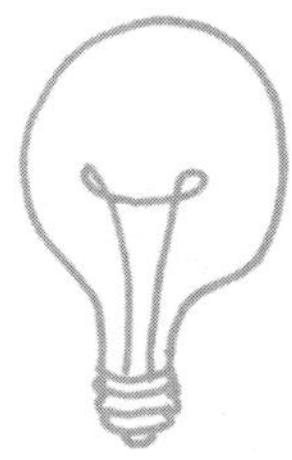

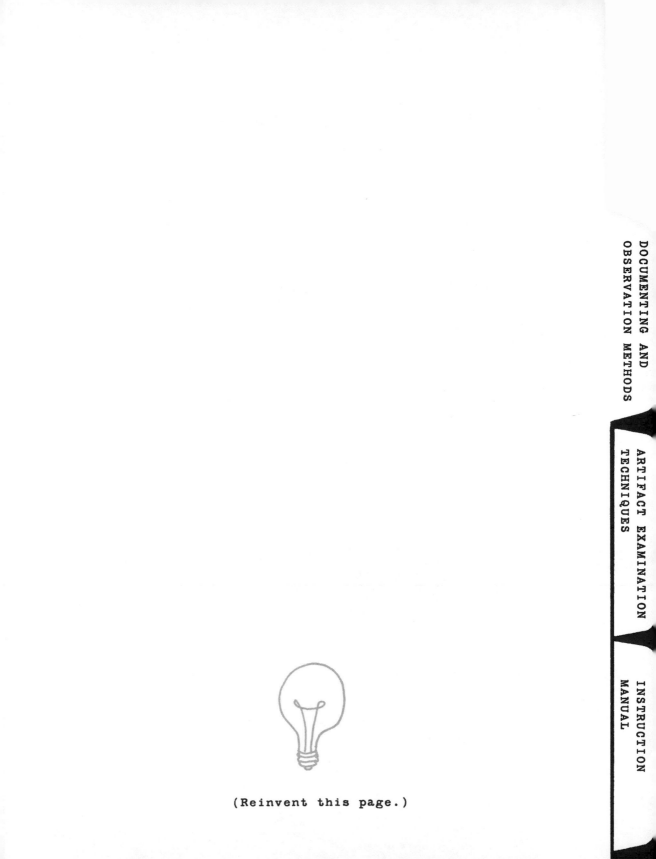

(Reinvent this page.)

DOCUMENTING AND OBSERVATION METHODS

OPERATION: CONDUCTING AN INTERVIEW

STATUS: ☐ IN PROGRESS ☐ COMPLETED

Consider talking to someone about this book. Who should you trust? Which friend do you think would be the most able to keep a secret? In order to determine this, it might help to ask your friends a few questions, to find out if they are trustworthy.

Conduct the interview to the left with chosen subjects.

INTERVIEW - Subject #1

What is your name, age, date of birth, and place of birth?

How many people are in your immediate family?

Do you consider yourself a trustworthy person?

Have you ever been in a situation where you found it necessary to lie?

Would you say you are good at keeping secrets?

INTERVIEW - Subject #2

What is your name, age, date of birth, and place of birth?

How many people are in your immediate family?

Do you consider yourself a trustworthy person?

Have you ever been in a situation where you found it necessary to lie?

Would you say you are good at keeping secrets?

DOCUMENTING AND OBSERVATION METHODS

OPERATION: DECEPTION METHODS 1

STATUS: ☐ IN PROGRESS ☐ COMPLETED

Put this book down. It seems the mystery of this manuscript and the Instruction Manual is going to take some time to uncover. This is a serious business. What if someone else recognizes it and knows that you are also on the quest to solve the mystery of the secret manual? It could be dangerous given that you know nothing about its origins. But what if you don't want to give it up? What if you want to complete the task you have been given? What if you want to finish this book?

A brilliant "lightbulb moment": Perhaps, like all great sleuths, you should engage in a few deception methods.

Create a disguise for this book so that no one will recognize it when you take it out in public. Delve to the depths of your creative genius to come up with a disguise. Document your results and write them here as a record of your mission progress.

Disguise Notes (possible configurations)

DOCUMENTING AND OBSERVATION METHODS

ARTIFACT EXAMINATION TECHNIQUES

INSTRUCTION MANUAL

DOCUMENTING AND OBSERVATION METHODS

OPERATION: DECEPTION METHODS 2

STATUS: ☐ IN PROGRESS ☐ COMPLETED

Just in case someone is following you, create a detailed fictitious character for you to pose as to lead them astray.

Write your fake bio on the right-hand page (include an altered photo of yourself in disguise, that is, draw over it).

NAME: INSPECTOR MOFFAT
OCCUPATION: PRIVATE INVESTIGATOR
LOCATION: MIDDLEBURY, VT
HOBBIES: COLLECTING PAPER, SPYING, CREATING DISGUISES
LIKES: SECRET DOCUMENTS, RARE BOOKS
DISLIKES: FACELESS CORPORATIONS, CONSUMERISM

PLACE
PHOTO
HERE

NAME:

DOB:

OCCUPATION:

LOCATION:

HOBBIES:

NICKNAME:

LIKES:

DISLIKES:

DOCUMENTING AND OBSERVATION METHODS

OPERATION: DISTRACTION TECHNIQUES

STATUS: ☐ IN PROGRESS ☐ COMPLETED

Come up with a list of tricks to distract potential followers (for example, confuse or annoy a perpetrator by sending them on an alternate route).

ARTIFACT EXAMINATION TECHNIQUES

OPERATION: LIST OF OBSERVATIONS

STATUS: ☐ IN PROGRESS ☐ COMPLETED

Now that you're safe in your disguise, it's time to examine the Instruction Manual.

When I found the abandoned pages in the park, I began to form several observations about them . . . things I could deduce by just looking at them, even though I didn't understand the content. In hindsight, I should have written down each of my observations because they were quite brilliant, and probably very relevant to the solving of the mystery. I fear that this task is left for you to complete now—it is my only hope.

Please write a detailed list of observations about the Instruction Manual.

List of Observations

TOP SECRET INFORMATION Please keep confidential.

ARTIFACT EXAMINATION TECHNIQUES

OPERATION: ABSTRACT THINKING

STATUS: ☐ IN PROGRESS ☐ COMPLETED

Think about the title of the found book: the Instruction Manual. Come up with a few ideas of what the book could be for, based on the title. Use your imagination for this exercise, it does not have to be based in reality. A good sleuth is able to think abstractly when necessary.

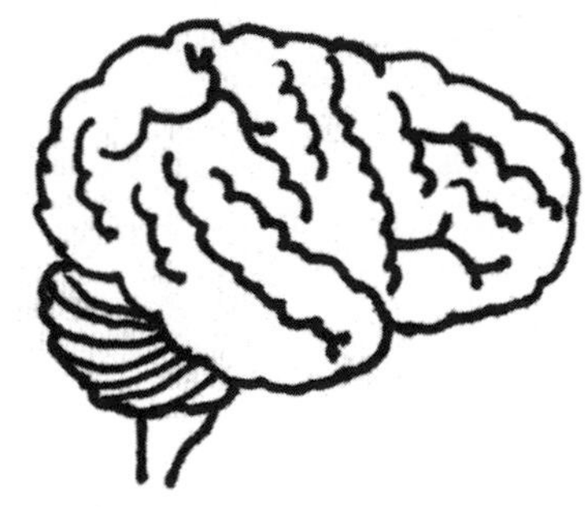

ARTIFACT EXAMINATION TECHNIQUES

OPERATION: IMAGERY INTERPRETATION

STATUS: ☐ IN PROGRESS ☐ COMPLETED

Think about the cover image of the found book.

What kind of message do you think the creator of the Instruction Manual is trying to communicate to us by using the symbol of a tree?

Draw a tree that is in your immediate environment.

(Draw a tree.)

ARTIFACT EXAMINATION TECHNIQUES

OPERATION: THEORY FORMULATION

STATUS: ☐ IN PROGRESS ☐ COMPLETED

Flip through the Instruction Manual, skimming through the pages, paying particular attention to the page numbers. It appears that pages 6 and 7 are missing.

What do you think happened to them?

6 & 7

ARTIFACT EXAMINATION TECHNIQUES

INSTRUCTION MANUAL

ARTIFACT EXAMINATION TECHNIQUES

OPERATION: GOOD LUCK SYMBOL

STATUS: ☐ IN PROGRESS ☐ COMPLETED

Is all this thinking wearing you out? It might be a good time for a diversion, a change of pace. Something to shift your mental state and reenergize you. It certainly couldn't hurt to ask for help in the form of a lucky talisman.

Research good luck symbols, and create your own. Draw it on the right-hand page.

(Draw a good luck symbol.)

ARTIFACT EXAMINATION TECHNIQUES

OPERATION: FINAL OPERATION

STATUS: ☐ IN PROGRESS ☐ COMPLETED

It has been a long day, and you have put in some hard work.

But come, it's getting dreadful late, you had better be turning flukes.

Research the above sentence to discover its meaning and source. Write them here.

PROCEED ONTO NEXT SECTION

While it is true there may be people who do not want this book to exist, you must continue with the task at hand. There is no telling what great work you will accomplish here, or what direction you will head in next. With every turn of the page, there is the promise of leaving behind the expected and the predictable.

You are now ready to work directly with the Instruction Manual and to begin solving its mystery.

"But I am not an expert sleuth," you think to yourself. "How do I know where to begin?"

That is a valid point. But you have just been trained as a sleuth, so you are ready to jump in. Besides, sometimes the only way to figure these things out is to simply move forward. Begin by turning the page.

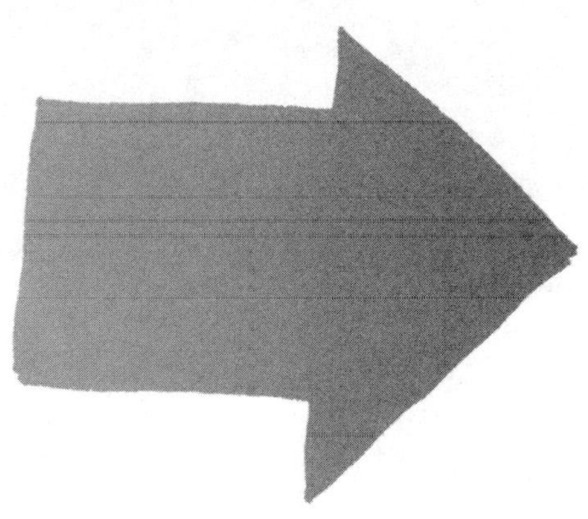

WHEN I FOUND THE INSTRUCTION MANUAL, IT WAS IN A RATHER FRAGILE STATE. MANY OF THE PAGES WERE DISINTEGRATING (SOME WERE BARELY LEGIBLE). SO I HAD TO WORK HARD TO INTERPRET MUCH OF THE WRITING. WHAT YOU READ HERE IS MY OWN INTERPRETATION OF THE ORIGINAL ARTIFACT AS BEST AS I COULD DECIPHER. —KS

YOUR MISSION

EXAMINE THE FOLLOWING PAGES. THEN, INTERPRET AND RE-CREATE THE PAGES IN YOUR OWN WAY. USE EVERYTHING YOU HAVE LEARNED SO FAR TO HELP TO "SOLVE" EACH PAGE.

PROCEED WITH CAUTION

ACCEPTANCE OF MISSION

YOUR SIGNATURE:

DATE:

FRONT
COVER

INSTRUCTION

MANUAL

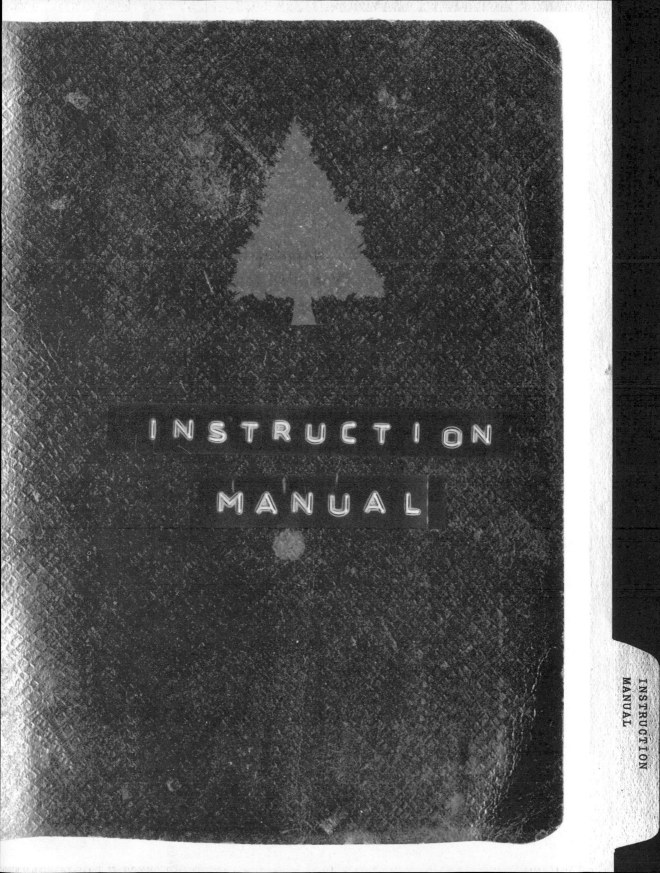

INSTRUCTION
MANUAL

NOTICE:
THIS BOOK REQUIRES YOUR IMMEDIATE ATTENTION.

THIS IS A BOOK BY **THE SECRET ORDER OF THE LOST FOREST.**

INSTRUCTION MANUAL

THE S.O.L.F. MANIFESTO

1. We declare the natural world as our playground in which every inch is to be explored and investigated.
2. In our explorations we promise to tread lightly on the earth.
3. We will attempt to pay attention to everything as if we have never seen it before.
4. We will use all of our senses during our travels.
5. We will not have a set agenda but remain open to the unexpected. (We will practice aimless wandering on a regular basis.)
6. We will pursue anything that piques our curiosity.
7. We will document our explorations.
8. We will incite our imagination as a means of reanimating the everyday world.
9. We will study and learn from all creatures we encounter.
10. We will come to understand that everything we see has a story.
11. We will make collections of things we find in the natural world in order to understand them better (while observing rule #2).
12. We have come to understand that the natural world is under threat by others who are damaging it. We of this secret order have chosen to take on the role of secret agent–fighting to care for the earth and attempting to teach others to do the same by sharing our ideas and findings (in a sometimes covert fashion).
13. We will share our symbol as one means of "spreading the word."
14. As explorers and sleuths we will find our own way of doing things.
15. And now we pass it on to you, to create your own order, to carry on our message or yours. Join the revolution.

HOW TO WRITE A MANIFESTO

A manifesto is a document you write that publicly declares your goals, rules, and dreams for your secret order. It is usually one page with bullet points (or in point form). Your manifesto will be read over and over again (to remind yourself and the group what you are striving for and to keep you on track with your goals).

1. Write about what you are passionate about. What do you stand for? What are your beliefs?

2. What gifts and ideas do you have to share with the world?

3. What big dreams do you have for your secret order? What would you like to accomplish? These can be serious goals, or they can be absurd (it's up to you).

4. Formulate a plan. Have some thoughts about how you might go about achieving those goals. (For example: if your goal is to have more members, you could create a poster inviting people.)

5. Research other manifestos and use some of the ideas you like.

6. Points can be as simple or complex as you like.

7. You may also add a list of Do's and Don'ts for your manifesto.

CREATE YOUR OWN BRANCH OF THE SECRET ORDER OF THE LOST FOREST. NAME IT HERE:

THE SECRET ______ OF THE ______.

(OTHER NAMES YOU MIGHT WANT TO USE FOR YOUR SECRET ORDER: GUILD, SOCIETY, LEAGUE, COOPERATIVE, FELLOWSHIP, CLUB, UNION, SISTERHOOD, BROTHERHOOD, PEOPLEHOOD, COLLECTIVE.)

WRITE A MANIFESTO FOR YOUR SECRET ORDER (OR ADD TO THE ONE IN THIS BOOK).

NOTE: YOU DO NOT HAVE TO HAVE A GROUP TO FORM A SECRET ORDER, YOU CAN CREATE A SECRET ORDER OF ONE.

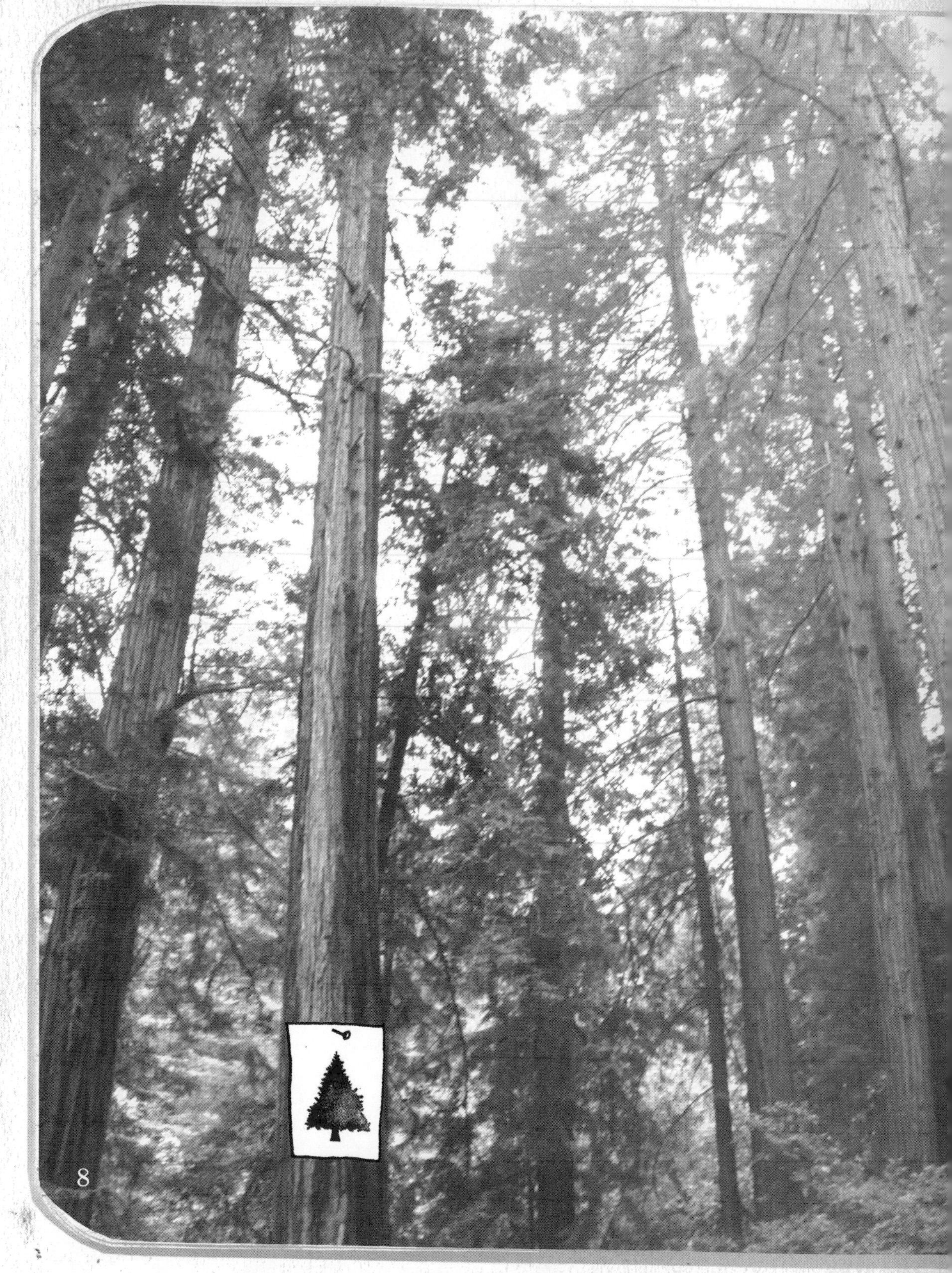

CREATE YOUR OWN SECRET HEADQUARTERS. THIS IS GOING TO BE HOME BASE FOR YOUR PERSONAL SECRET ORDER.

FIND A PLACE THAT SPEAKS TO YOU AND FEELS GOOD FOR YOU TO SPEND LOTS OF TIME. THIS COULD BE A SIMPLE SITTING SPOT OUTSIDE THAT NO ONE ELSE KNOWS ABOUT SOMEWHERE NEAR YOUR HOUSE. MAYBE YOU LIKE IT TO FEEL "HIDDEN" OR SECLUDED. TRY A PLACE THAT HAS LOTS OF NATURE AND WILDLIFE TO OBSERVE SO YOU CAN CONDUCT THE EXPLORATIONS IN THIS MANUAL. IT WOULD BE GOOD IF THE PLACE IS A BIT SHELTERED FROM WEATHER, SOMEWHERE YOU CAN SIT FOR LONG PERIODS, AND SOMEWHERE YOU FEEL COMFORTABLE. YOU WILL GET TO KNOW THIS PLACE VERY WELL. IT WILL HOPEFULLY BECOME A GOOD "FRIEND" TO YOU.

YOU MAY WISH TO DECORATE IT IN A SUBTLE WAY (NOT TOO MUCH OR OTHERS WILL BE ABLE TO IDENTIFY IT). HIDE SOME THINGS THERE. CREATE A SECRET HISTORY OF YOUR SPOT.

Secret Headquarters

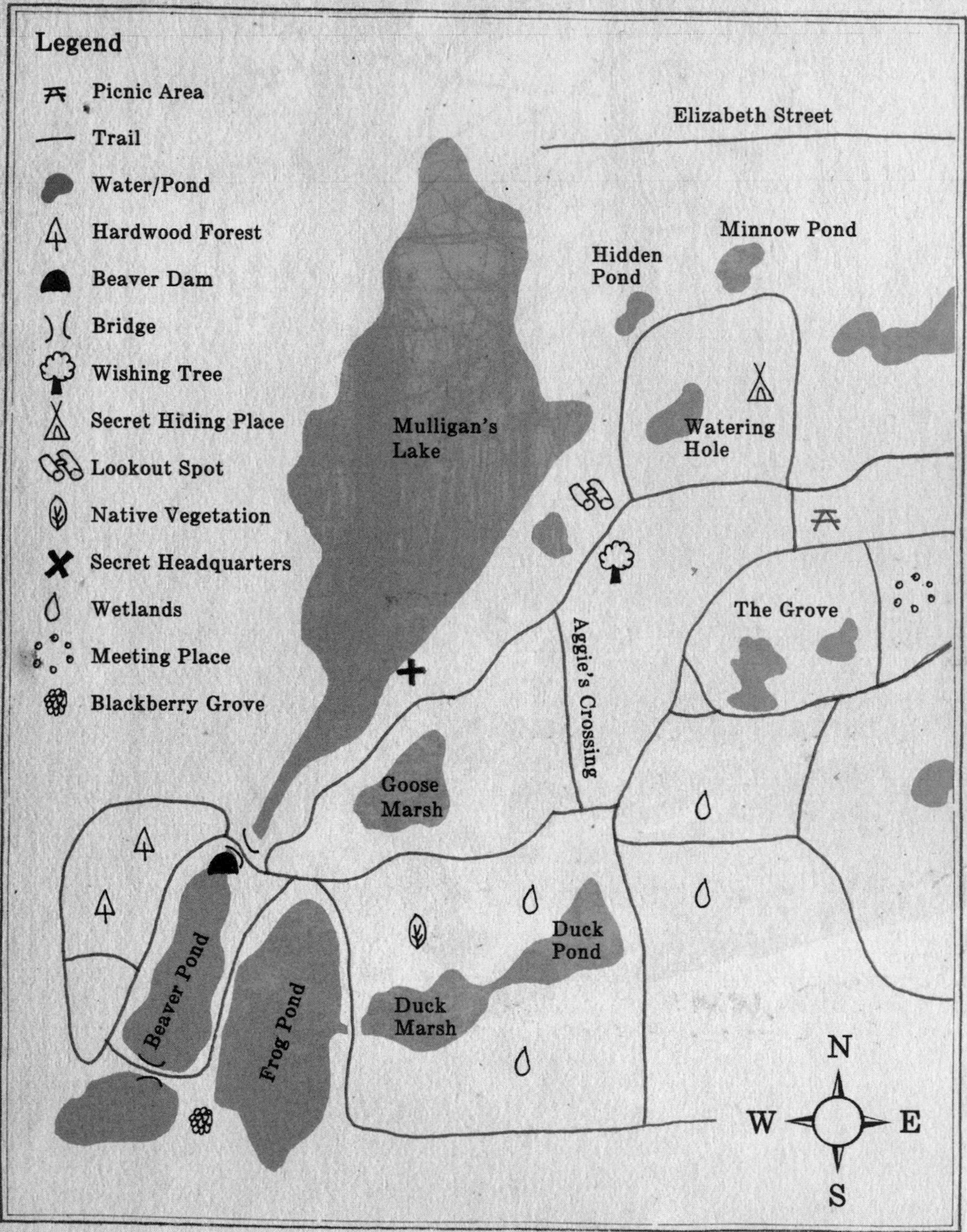
Legend
Picnic Area
Trail
Water/Pond
Hardwood Forest
Beaver Dam
Bridge
Wishing Tree
Secret Hiding Place
Lookout Spot
Native Vegetation
Secret Headquarters
Wetlands
Meeting Place
Blackberry Grove
Elizabeth Street
Minnow Pond
Hidden Pond
Mulligan's Lake
Watering Hole
The Grove
Aggie's Crossing
Goose Marsh
Duck Pond
Duck Marsh
Beaver Pond
Frog Pond
N
W
E
S

CREATE A DETAILED MAP OF YOUR SECRET HEADQUARTERS LOCATION. INCLUDE LANDMARKS, TREES, WILDLIFE, AND TYPES OF VEGETATION. INCLUDE COMPASS DIRECTIONS.

The Arch of Invincibility
All who pass under this
arch are given a secret
power that lasts for
several hours.

LOOKING AT THE MAP YOU CREATED OF YOUR SECRET LOCATION, DEVISE IMAGINARY STORIES ABOUT THE LANDMARKS IN AND AROUND YOUR SECRET HEADQUARTERS. WHAT IF SOME LANDMARKS HAD SECRET POWERS? WHAT WOULD THEY BE?

Fox
Snake
Owl
Eagle
Beaver
Robin
Moose
Hare
Turtle

CHOOSE AN ANIMAL TO USE AS A MASCOT FOR YOUR SECRET ORDER. STUDY CHARACTERISTICS OF DIFFERENT ANIMALS, AND PICK ONE THAT SUITS YOUR PERSONALITY.

FIND IMAGERY OF THIS ANIMAL. CREATE A THREE-DIMENSIONAL VERSION OUT OF WHATEVER MATERIAL YOU HAVE ON HAND.

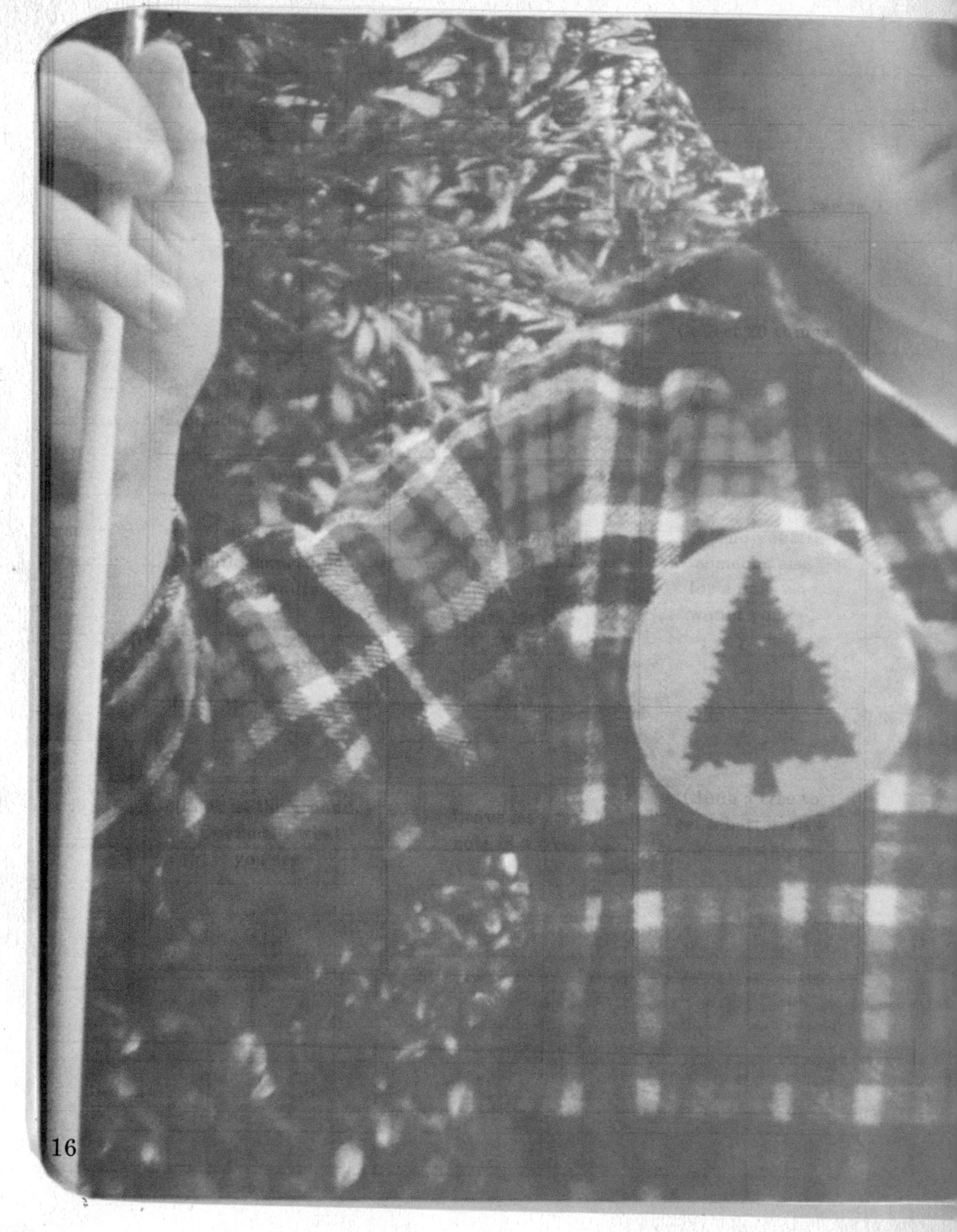

CREATE SOME KIND OF WEARABLE ITEM FOR THE SECRET ORDER SO THAT OTHERS WILL BE ABLE TO IDENTIFY YOU. THIS WILL BE PART OF YOUR "UNIFORM." YOU MAY CHOOSE TO COLLECT SOME ITEMS FROM YOUR SECRET LOCATION TO USE (SUCH AS ROCKS OR LEAVES). KEEP IT ON YOUR BODY AT ALL TIMES.

SOME IDEAS:

PIN / BROOCH
BRACELET
NECKLACE
RING
BARRETTE
T-SHIRT
SOMETHING KNITTED

1. Names of places you would like to explore.	2. Names of other explorers you would like to learn about.	3. Names of animals you would like to spot.
4. Names of books you want to find.	5. Names of items you would like to collect.	6. Names of places explored so far.
7. Names of items you have found.	8. Names of things you have seen at your headquarters.	9. Names of things you've hidden.
10. Names of sounds you've heard.	11. Names of plants, trees, birds, and bugs you've identified.	12. Names of smells you've smelled.

WHILE SITTING AT YOUR SECRET HEADQUARTERS, ADD TO THE LIST ON THE LEFT AS YOU UNCOVER THINGS.

READ A BOOK AT YOUR SECRET HEADQUARTERS.

SHARE A PASSAGE FROM THE BOOK.
REWRITE IT HERE.

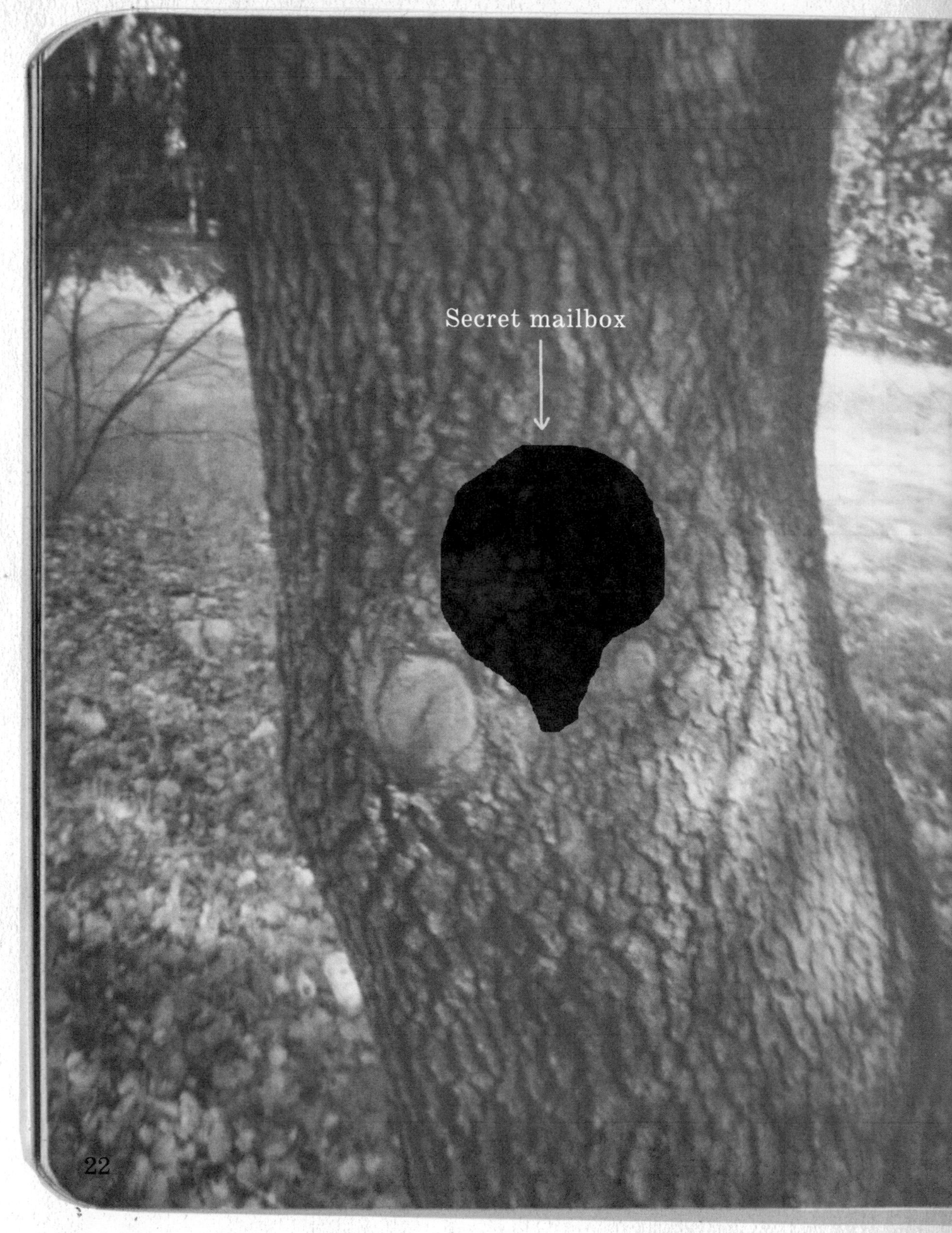
Secret mailbox

SELECT A TREE IN THE VICINITY OF YOUR SECRET HEADQUARTERS. GET TO KNOW THIS TREE. STUDY ITS LEAVES, BARK, AND BRANCHES. CAN YOU IDENTIFY WHAT KIND OF TREE IT IS? USE YOUR SENSES. TOUCH IT WITH YOUR EYES CLOSED. BREAK THE LEAVES AND SMELL THEM. LISTEN TO THE SOUNDS THE TREE MAKES. GIVE THE TREE A NAME. SEE IF THERE ARE ANY NESTS IN THE TREE. DOES IT BEAR FRUIT OR NUTS? WHO ELSE VISITS THE TREE? ARE THERE HIDING PLACES IN IT? CREATE YOUR OWN CODED MESSAGE AND LEAVE IT IN THE TREE. WOULD YOUR TREE SHELTER YOU IN THE RAIN? DOCUMENT THE TREE AT DIFFERENT TIMES OF THE YEAR. IF THIS TREE WERE A SPIRIT, WHAT WOULD ITS PERSONALITY BE LIKE?

TREE STUMP WITH ROCKS
Meaning: Meet me at the Secret Headquarters.

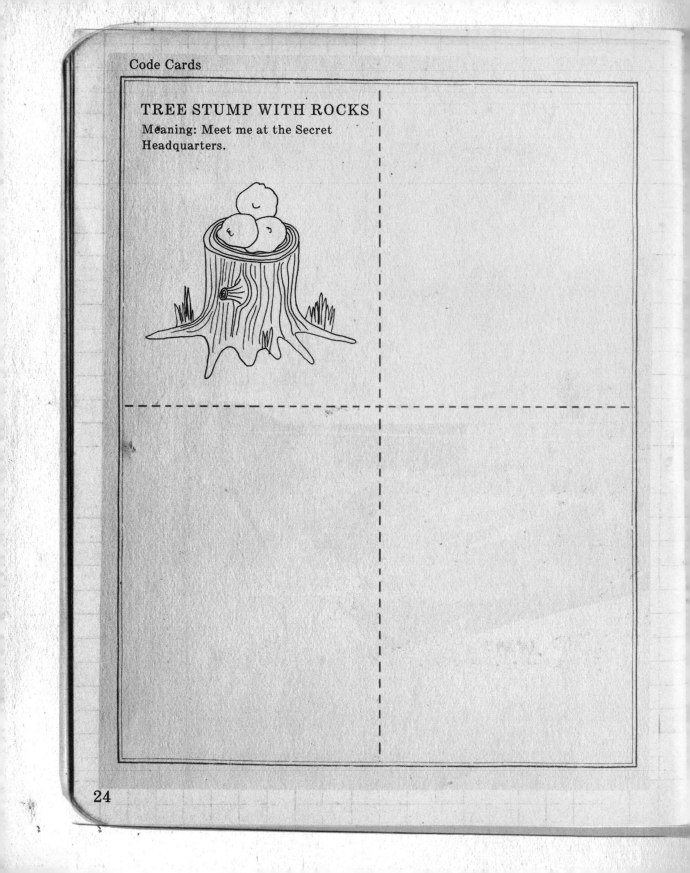

CREATE YOUR OWN CODES (OR SIGNS THAT COMMUNICATE THINGS TO OTHER PEOPLE IN YOUR SECRET ORDER). FOR EXAMPLE, A PILE OF ROCKS LETS SOMEONE KNOW THAT YOU ARE WAITING FOR THEM AT A PREDETERMINED LOCATION. CREATE A SECRET HANDSHAKE. CREATE YOUR OWN CODE NAME. CREATE YOUR OWN CALL (A SOUND USED TO GATHER OTHERS TO YOUR LOCATION).

TAKE A PORTRAIT OF YOURSELF IN YOUR SECRET HEADQUARTERS IN WHICH YOUR FACE IS HIDDEN.

ALTERNATIVE: IS IT POSSIBLE TO BLEND INTO THE LANDSCAPE? REMAIN HIDDEN SO YOU ARE UNDETECTED BY OTHERS? HOW CAN YOU BE INVISIBLE? COME UP WITH A FEW WAYS OF DOING THIS.

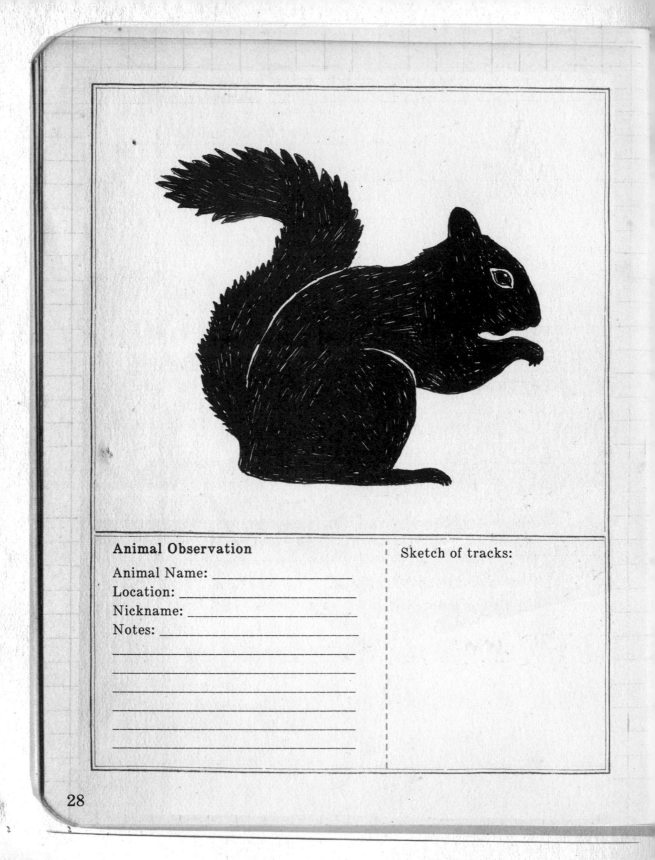

Animal Observation

Animal Name: ____________________

Location: ________________________

Nickname: ________________________

Notes: ___________________________

____

____

____

____

____

____

Sketch of tracks:

OBSERVE AN ANIMAL WHO VISITS YOUR SECRET HEADQUARTERS. TAKE NOTES ON ITS BEHAVIOR, MOVEMENT, AND TRAITS. TRY TO IMAGINE WHAT IT WOULD BE LIKE TO BE THAT ANIMAL. HOW WOULD IT SEE THE WORLD? HOW IS ITS VIEWPOINT DIFFERENT THAN YOURS?

MUSEUM OPEN
~ TODAY ~
Hours: by chance

FIND A "SHELF" SOMEWHERE NEAR YOUR SECRET HEADQUARTERS. IT COULD BE A TREE BRANCH, OR A HOLE IN A TREE, OR JUST A LARGE, FLAT ROCK. USE IT TO DISPLAY SOME ITEMS YOU HAVE FOUND AS A KIND OF OUTDOOR MUSEUM. CREATE A MAP SHOWING WHERE YOU FOUND THE VARIOUS ITEMS.

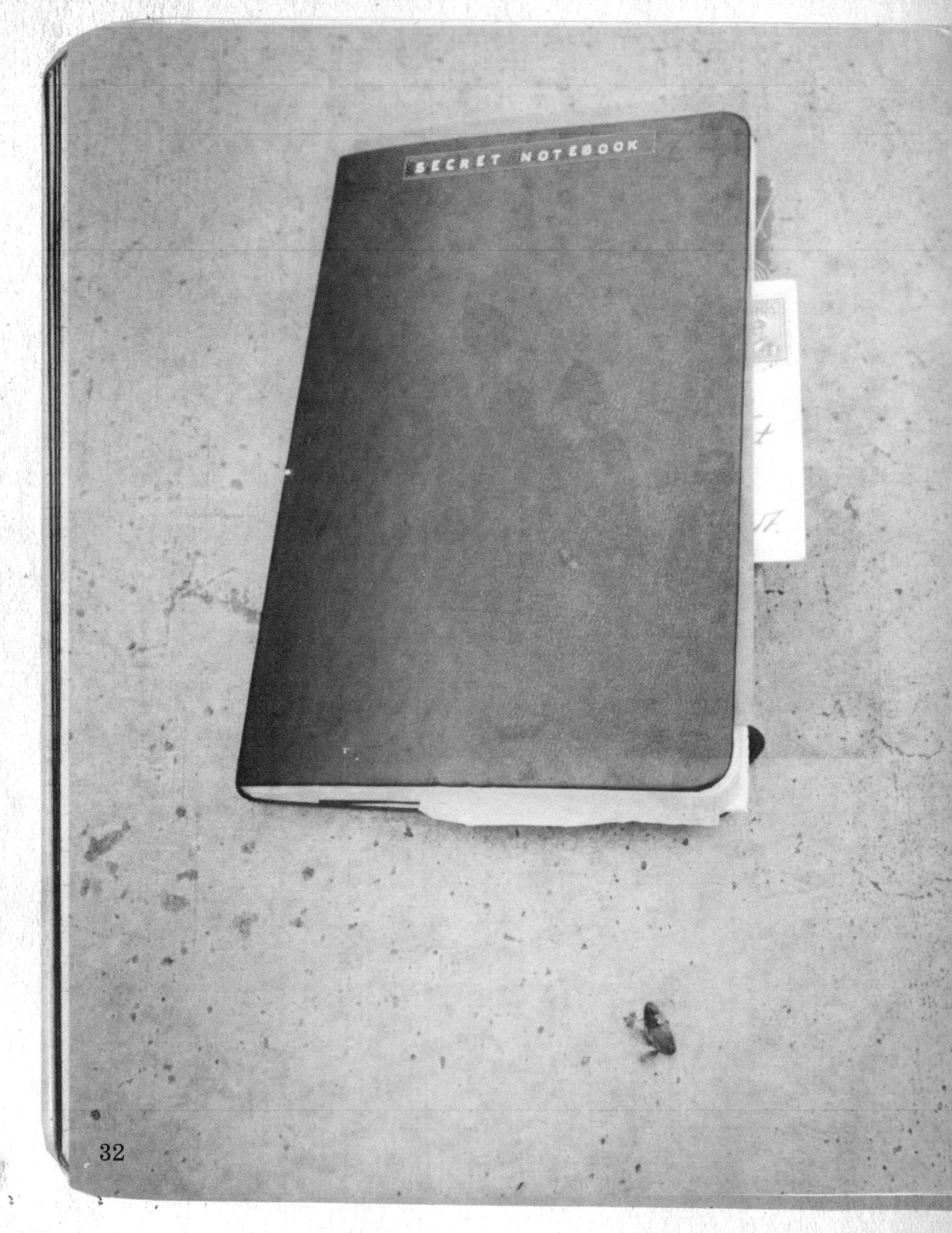
SECRET NOTEBOOK

JOURNALING

SIT IN YOUR SECRET HEADQUARTERS. DOCUMENT EVERYTHING YOU SEE IN ONE HOUR.

SOME THINGS TO WRITE ABOUT:

- DATE, TIME, LOCATION, DIRECTION (COMPASS LOCATION).
- HOW IS THE WEATHER?
- WHAT WILDLIFE CAN YOU SPOT?
- LOCATION OF THE SUN OR MOON OR STARS WHEN YOU ARRIVE AND WHEN YOU LEAVE.
- FIND SOMETHING IN THE AREA THAT INTERESTS YOU AND WRITE ABOUT IT.

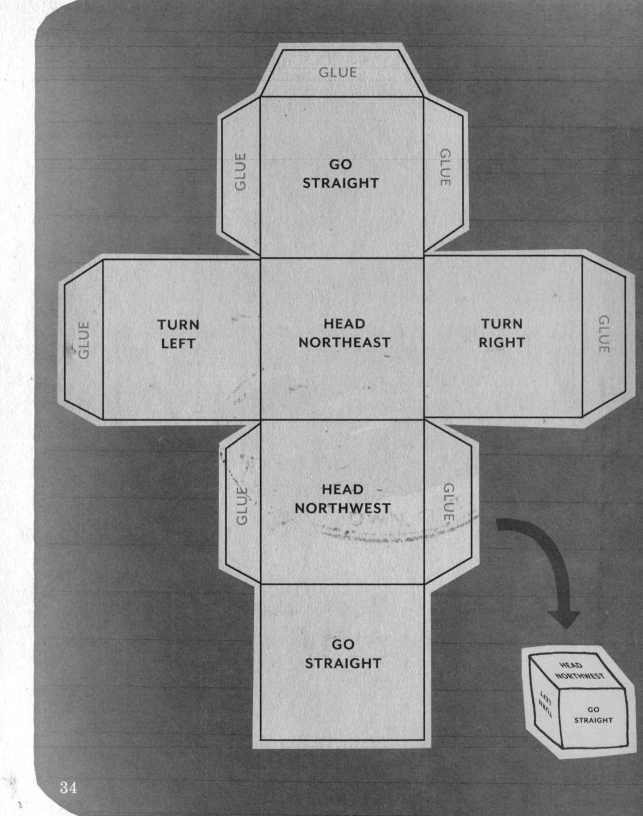

GLUE

GLUE

GO
STRAIGHT

GLUE

GLUE

TURN
LEFT

HEAD
NORTHEAST

TURN
RIGHT

GLUE

GLUE

HEAD
NORTHWEST

GLUE

GO
STRAIGHT

HEAD
NORTHWEST

TURN
LEFT

GO
STRAIGHT

NOW IT IS TIME TO VENTURE OUT OF YOUR SECRET HEADQUARTERS.

THIS PAGE SEEMS TO BE ASKING YOU TO TAKE A JOURNEY OF SORTS. YOU WILL USE IT TO EXPLORE THE NATURAL WORLD VIA AIMLESS WANDERING. START AT YOUR SECRET HEADQUARTERS. ROLL THE DIE. TAKE FIVE STEPS IN THE DIRECTION INDICATED. CONTINUE ROLLING THE DIE. DOCUMENT YOUR MOVEMENT. WHERE DO YOU END UP?

INSTRUCTION MANUAL

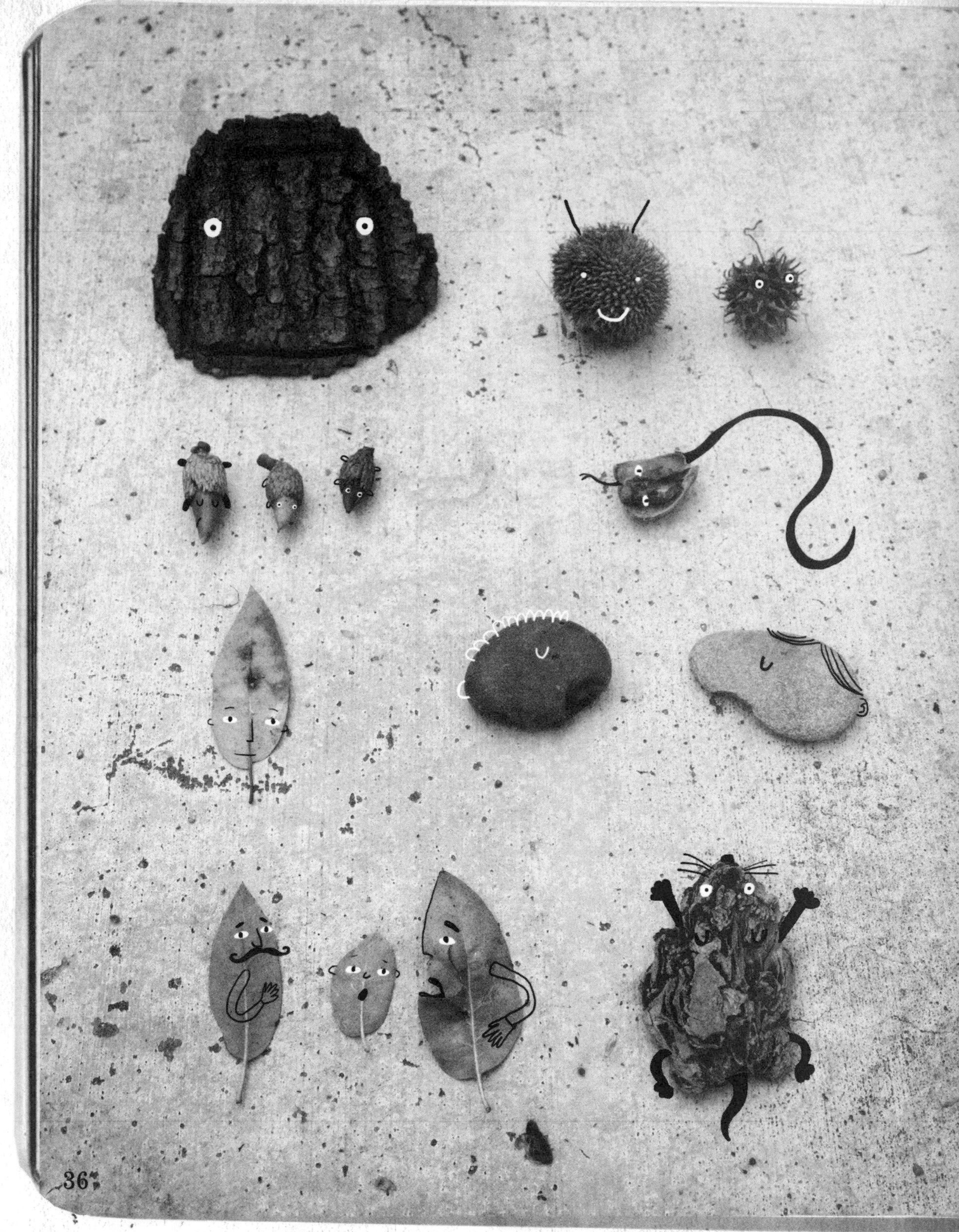

CREATE A SERIES OF CHARACTERS OUT OF THINGS YOU FIND AROUND YOUR SECRET HEADQUARTERS. USE A PEN OR MARKER TO HELP CREATE FACES OR DETAILS. LEAVE THESE "CREATURES" IN LOCATIONS WHERE PEOPLE MIGHT SEE THEM.

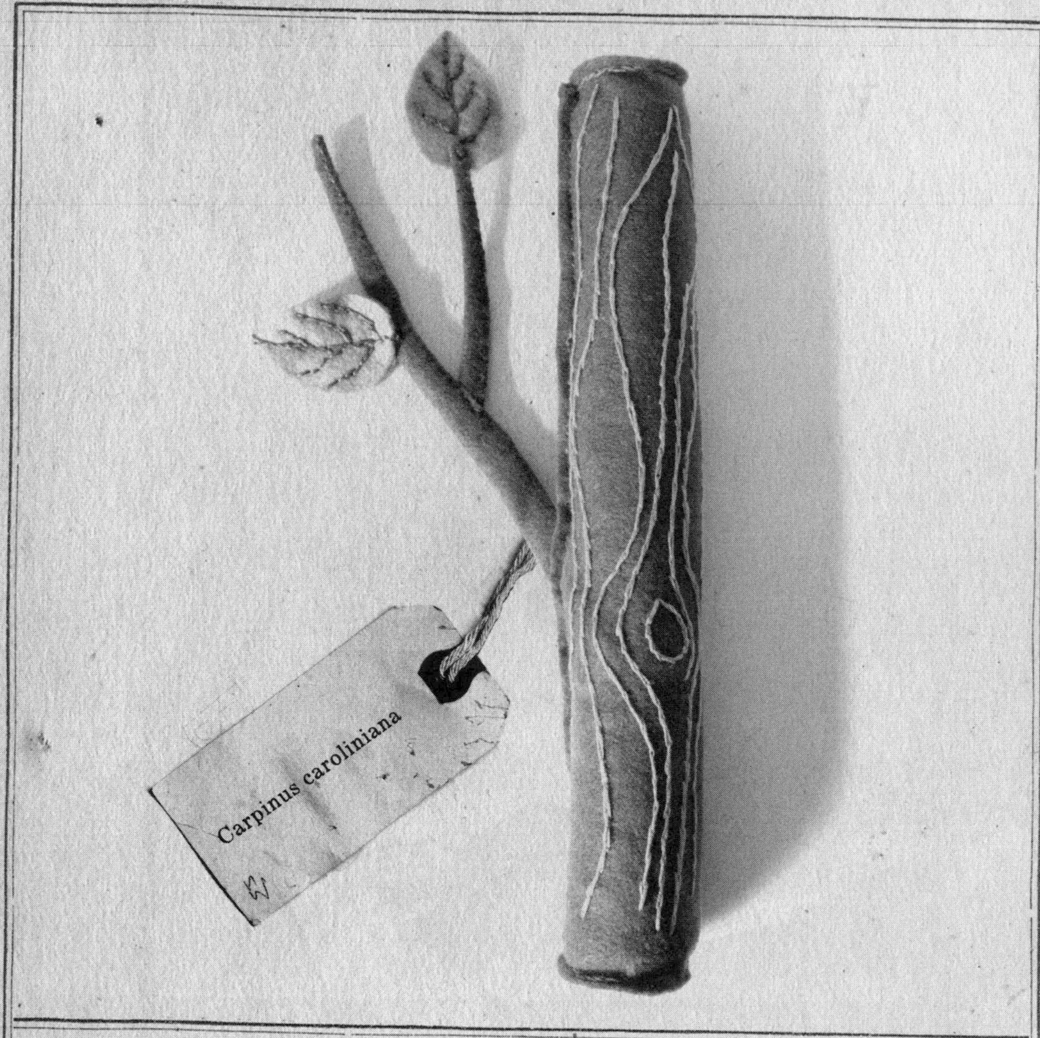

Tree Sample

Kingdom: Plantae
Division: Magnoliophyta
Class: Magnoliopsida
Order: Fagales
Family: Betulaceae (birch family)
Genus species: Carpinus caroliniana

Leaves: 5 to 11 cm long, 2.5 to 6 cm wide. Elliptical in shape, long-pointed at tip. Double-toothed veins are prominent.
Bark: Smooth bark, blue gray color. Bark has a sinewy look, like muscles.

FIND SOMETHING FROM THE NATURAL WORLD. RE-CREATE IT USING A DIFFERENT MATERIAL. FOR EXAMPLE, CREATE A SPIDER'S WEB OUT OF STRING, MAKE A FLY'S WING OUT OF PAPER CLIPS, OR MAKE A PATCH OF GRASS OUT OF PAPER AND CARDBOARD. TRY TO MAKE IT AS CLOSE TO THE ORIGINAL AS POSSIBLE.

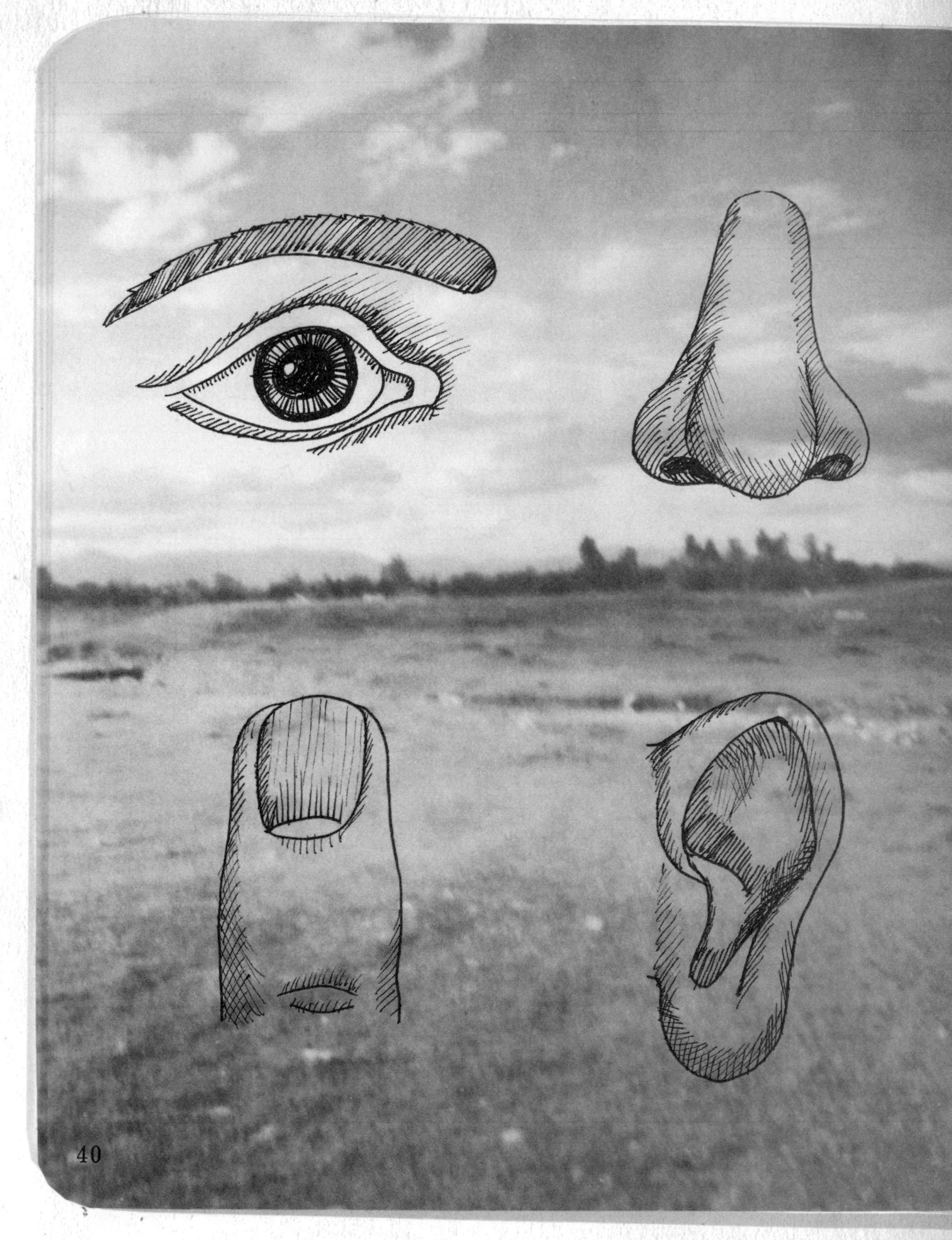

EXPLORE A PLACE YOU ARE FAMILIAR WITH IN NEW WAYS. DOCUMENT YOUR RESULTS. (VARIOUS METHODS OF EXPLORATION INCLUDE CLOSING YOUR EYES AND USING YOUR HANDS, YOUR NOSE, AND YOUR EARS.)

INSTRUCTION MANUAL

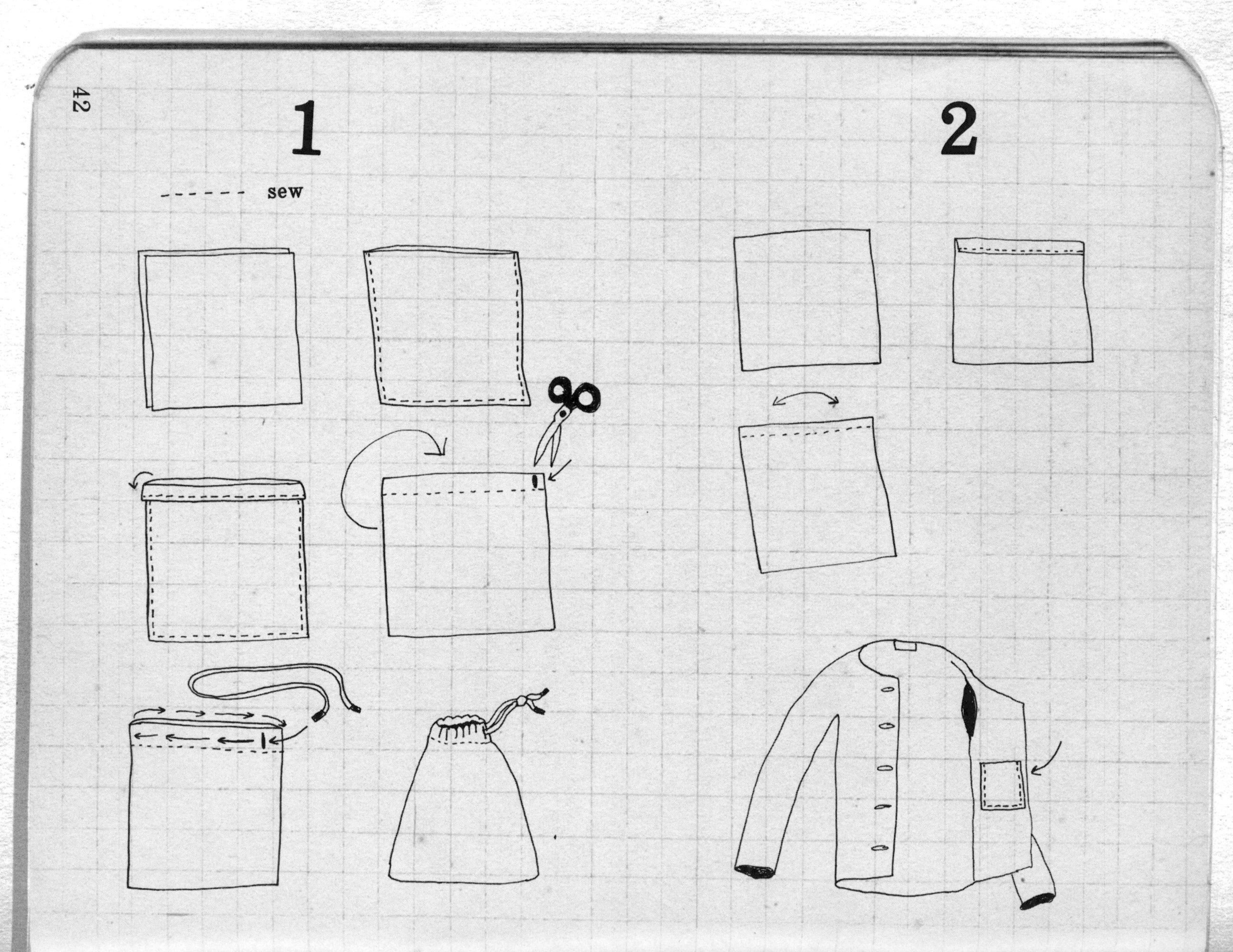
1
sew
2

USING ONE OF THE METHODS HERE (BAG OR SECRET POCKET), CREATE YOUR OWN COLLECTION DEVICE.

SCAVENGER HUNT

CREATE YOUR OWN VERSION OF THIS PAGE.
COLLECT THINGS YOU FIND INTERESTING.
FIND A WAY TO DISPLAY THEM.

SIT IN A PLACE THAT IS GOOD FOR PEOPLE WATCHING. TRY TO REMAIN UNDETECTED. A GOOD TRACKER WHO NO ONE CAN SEE BUT WHO SEES ALL. TAKE NOTES AND CREATE IMAGINARY BIOGRAPHIES FOR THE PEOPLE YOU WATCH.

Mr. Jeeves's House

CREATE YOUR OWN SMALL IMAGINARY WORLD OUT OF WHATEVER YOU HAVE LYING AROUND. PLACE IT IN A NATURAL SETTING.

DRAW OR PHOTOGRAPH YOUR HAND.

WHAT HAS THIS HAND TOUCHED IN ITS LIFETIME?

STUDY A FAMOUS NATURE EXPLORER. MAKE THIS PERSON INTO A GUIDE OF SORTS. RE-CREATE SOME OF THEIR ADVENTURES IN YOUR OWN NEIGHBORHOOD.

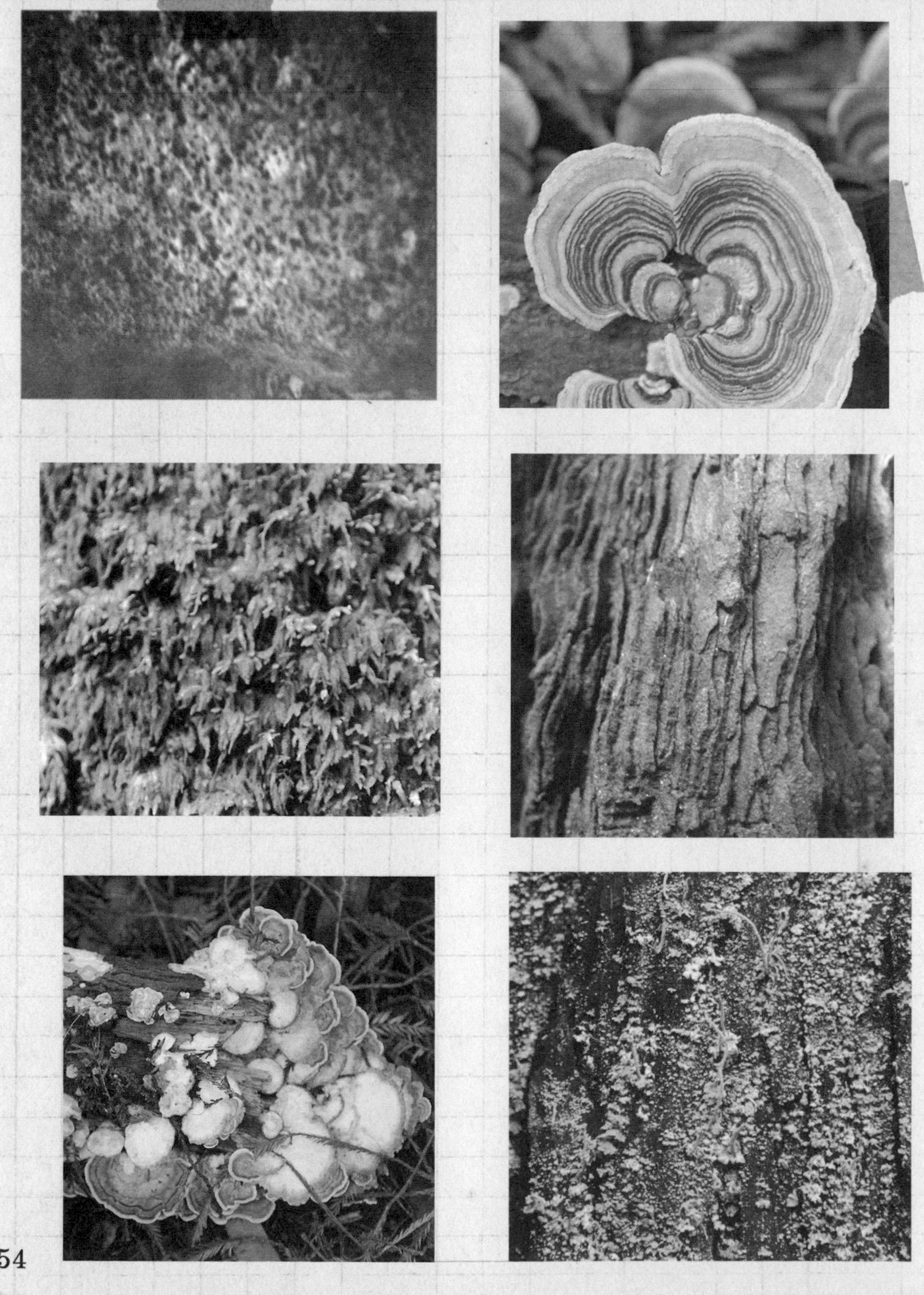

FIND AS MANY DIFFERENT PATTERNS IN NATURE AS YOU CAN.

COLLECT PAPER OR PAPER-LIKE MATERIALS (LIKE LEAVES). CREATE A SMALL NOTEBOOK WITH THEM. IT DOES NOT HAVE TO BE A FUNCTIONAL NOTEBOOK; IT CAN ALSO BE A COLLECTION OF SORTS.

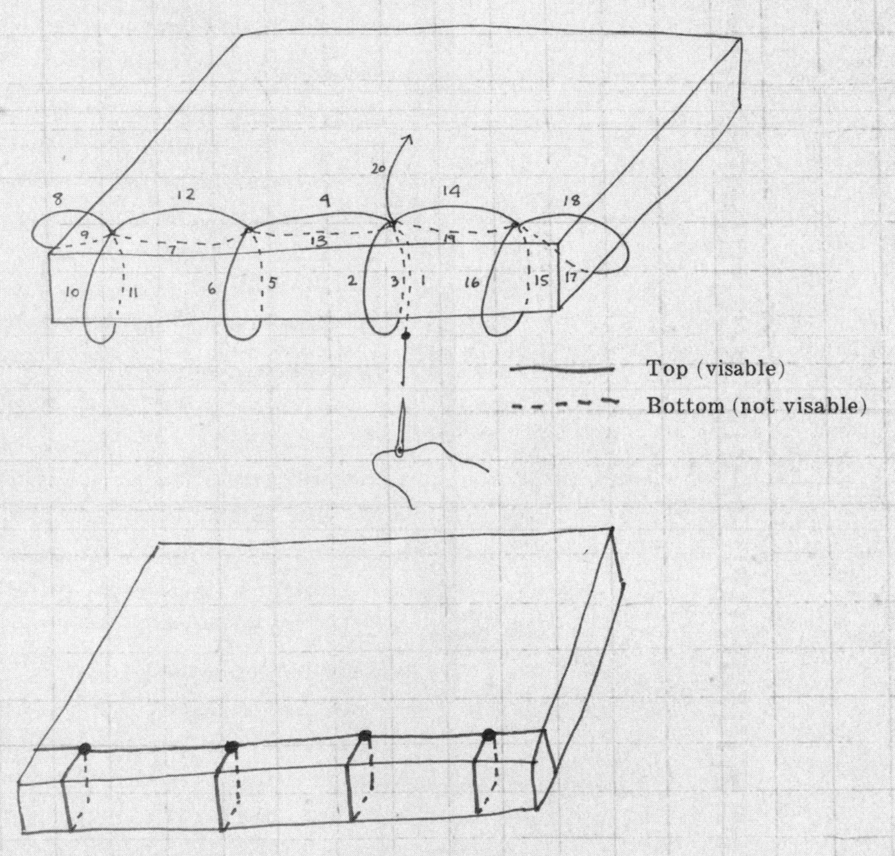

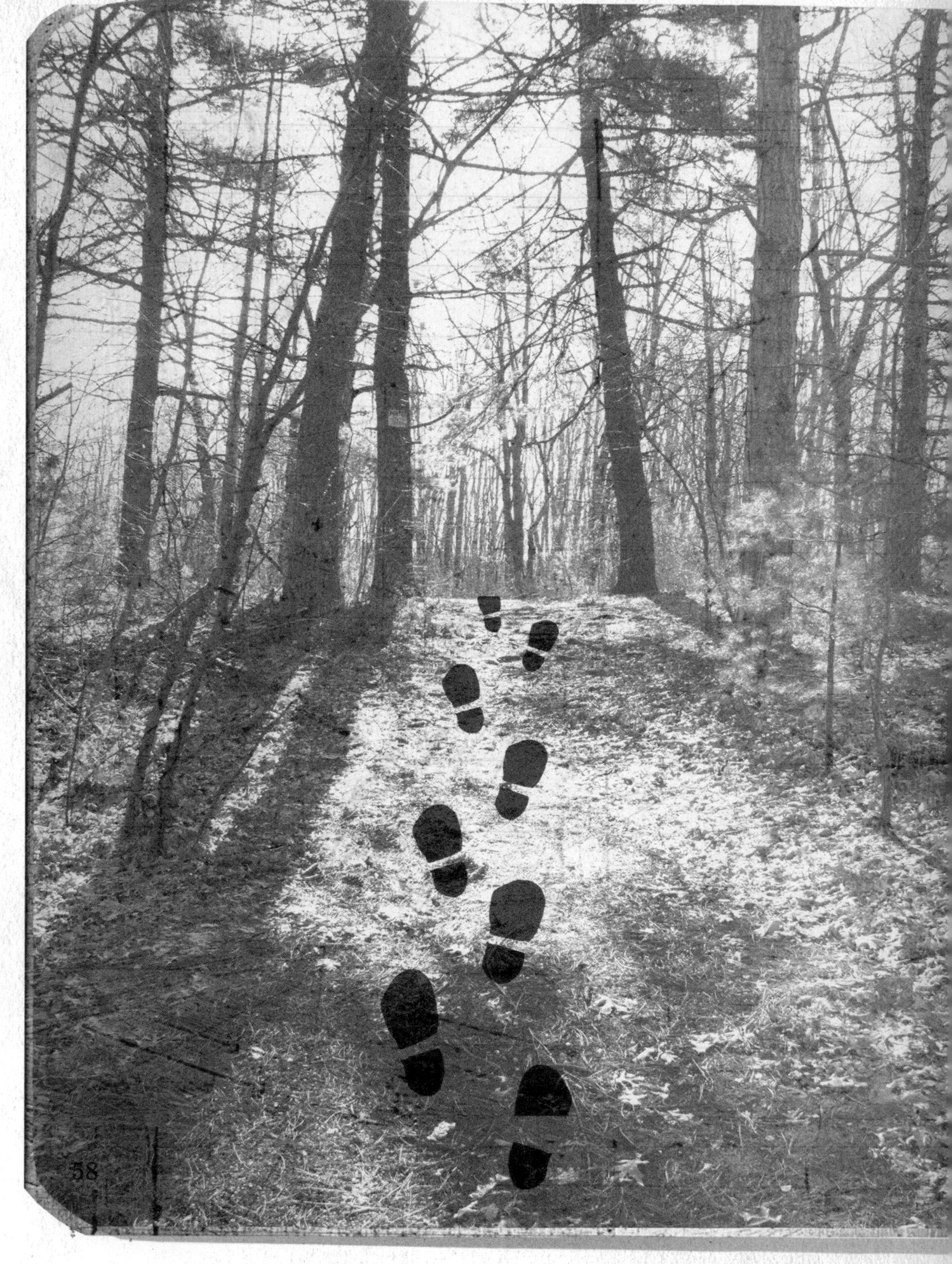

LEAVE A TRAIL OF SOME KIND ON PURPOSE. YOU MAY WISH TO HAVE A FRIEND TRACK YOU TO YOUR SECRET HEADQUARTERS. YOU CAN USE A VARIETY OF METHODS: FOOTPRINTS, STONE PILES, CHALK ARROWS ON TREES, STRING, ETC.

IF YOU HAVE A CAMERA, GO "HUNTING" WITH IT TO SEE WHAT YOU CAN DOCUMENT. (IF YOU DON'T HAVE ONE, WRITE NOTES ABOUT WHAT YOU CAN SEE.) WHAT DO YOU SEE? WHAT IMAGE WOULD YOU LIKE TO SHARE WITH OTHERS? DESCRIBE IT.

IF FOUND DO NOT OPEN

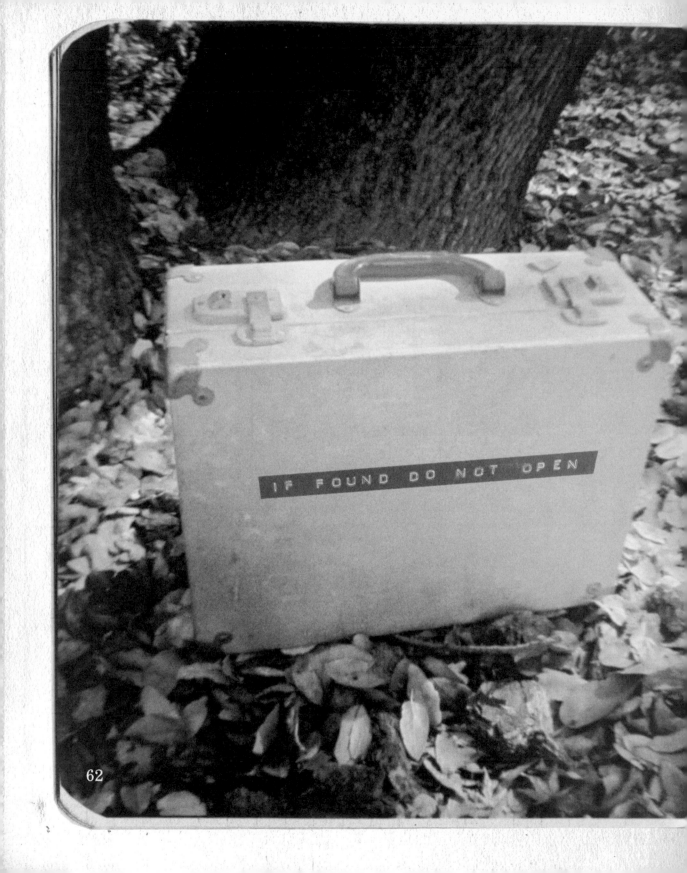

FIND SOME KIND OF WEATHERPROOF BOX. FILL IT WITH ITEMS USED BY YOUR SECRET ORDER (COPIES OF MAPS, YOUR MANIFESTO, DRAWINGS, COLLECTED ITEMS, ETC.). BURY IT IN A SECRET LOCATION. CREATE A TREASURE MAP TO MARK ITS LOCATION IN CASE YOU FORGET WHERE IT IS.

Get lost.	Sit in one place for 10 minutes.	Collect 20 things.
Build something in 10 minutes.	Pick up something within 2 feet of you. Come up with 20 uses for it.	Pretend you are someone else for a day–who would you be?
Look at the ground. Document what you see.	Leave a secret note in a tree.	Climb a tree to get a better view of something.

DROP A COIN OR A ROCK ONTO THIS PAGE.
FOLLOW INSTRUCTIONS.

SPEND SOME TIME WATCHING THE SKY.
DOCUMENT IT IN SOME WAY.

Plate 46

Black	White	Blue
Red	Brown	Yellow
Orange	Dark green	Olive green
Gray	Rust	Cream

FIND EXAMPLES OF ALL THESE COLORS IN NATURE. COLLECT SAMPLES IF POSSIBLE. ATTACH NOTES ABOUT WHERE THE SAMPLES WERE FOUND.

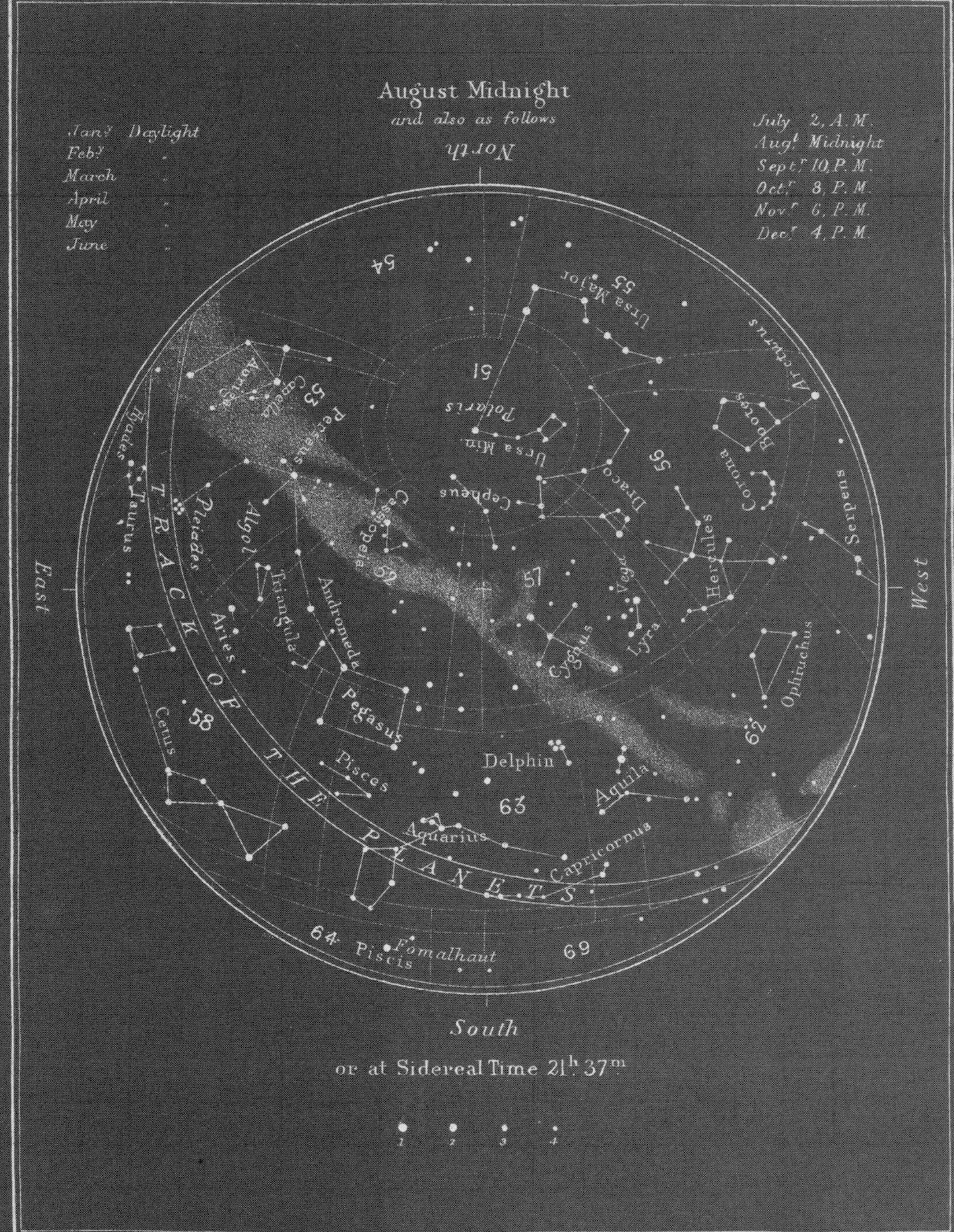

George Philip & Son, London & Liverpool.

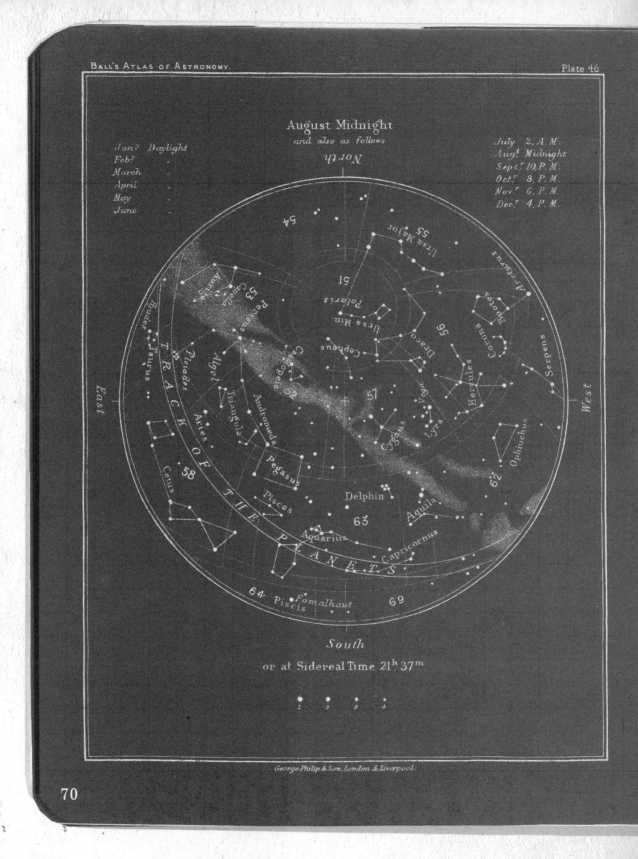

"LET US GO THEN, YOU AND I, WHEN THE EVENING IS SPREAD OUT AGAINST THE SKY."

—T. S. ELIOT

TRACK THE MOVEMENT OF THE SUN AND MOON WHERE YOU LIVE. RECORD IT HERE.

3737

YOU HAVE IMMENSE POWERS.
REPURPOSE THIS EMPTY LOT.
TRANSFORM IT INTO SOMETHING
THAT WILL HELP THE PLANET.

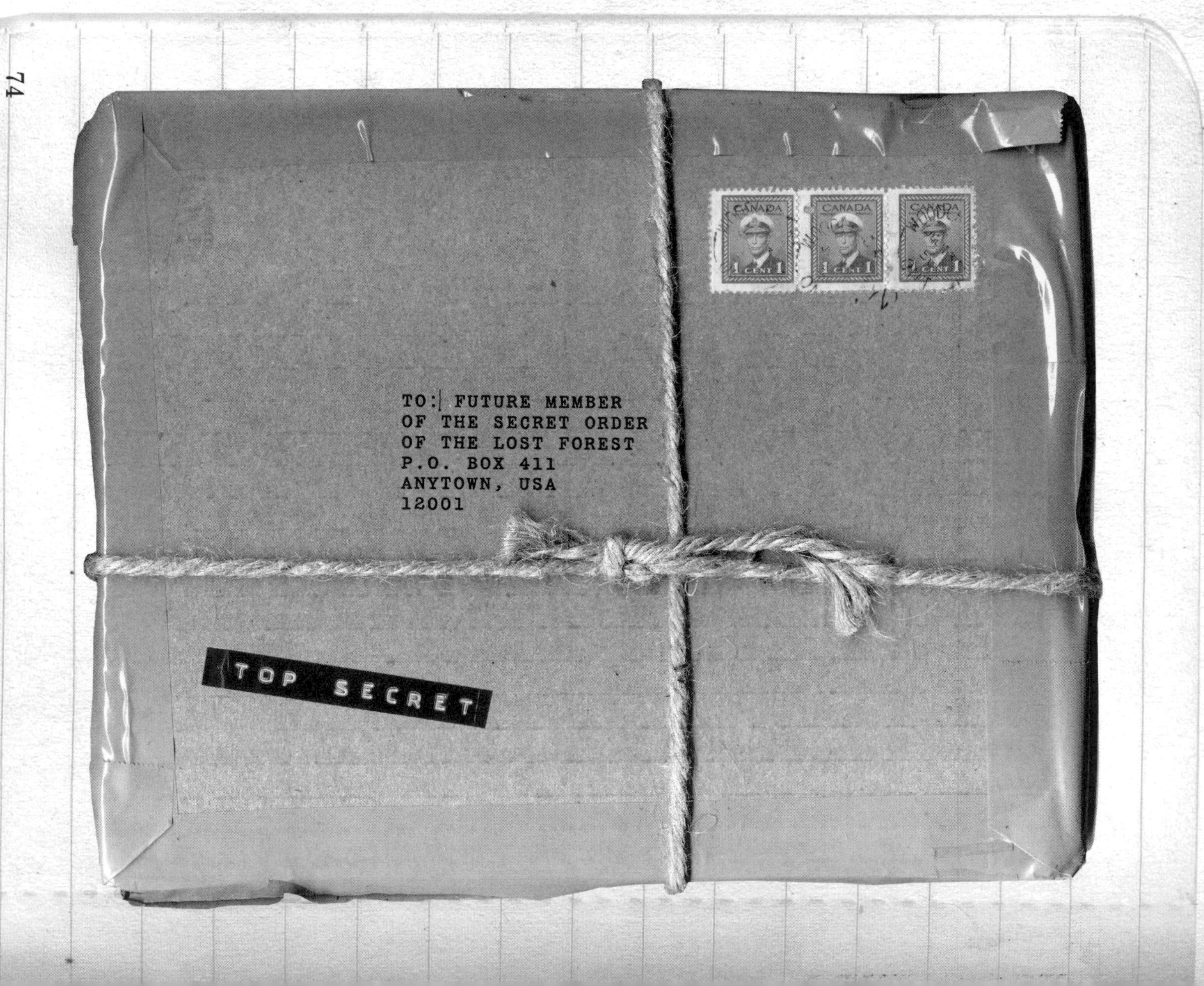
CANADA 1 CENT
CANADA 1 CENT
CANADA 1 CENT
TO: FUTURE MEMBER
OF THE SECRET ORDER
OF THE LOST FOREST
P.O. BOX 411
ANYTOWN, USA
12001
TOP SECRET

SEND A LETTER INVITING SOMEONE TO JOIN YOUR SECRET ORDER. YOU MAY WISH TO CREATE YOUR OWN STATIONERY FOR THIS PURPOSE. INCLUDE SOME INTERESTING RANDOM ITEMS THAT YOU'VE COLLECTED IN THE ENVELOPE.

ALTERNATE: IF YOU DON'T WISH TO INVITE OTHERS TO JOIN YOUR SECRET ORDER, YOU CAN MAIL A COPY OF YOUR MANIFESTO TO YOURSELF AS A WAY OF FORMALLY PUBLISHING AND DOCUMENTING YOUR SECRET ORDER. THE MAIL PROVIDES A DATING STAMP THAT WILL MAKE THE MANIFESTO AN "OFFICIAL" DOCUMENT.

Meeting Agenda

Secret Order of the Lost Forest
Branch: ____________________
Meeting Purpose: ____________________
Location: ____________________
Date/Time: ____________________

Agenda

1. Role call.
2. Reading of the manifesto.
3. Ideas and suggestions.
4. Activities:

-badge creation
-fundraising methods
-nature games
-scavenger hunt
-skill sharing
-community outreach

____
____
____
____
____
____
____

5. Break (snacks & refreshments).
6. Closing remarks.
7. Next meeting notes.
8. Secret handshake.
9. Clean up.

Meeting Action Items

(job assignments)

Name: ____________________
Action: ____________________

Name: ____________________
Action: ____________________

Name: ____________________
Action: ____________________

Meeting Follow-Up

Next Meeting Date: ____________________
____
Location: ____________________
Notes: ____________________
____
____

DEVISE A MEETING FOR YOUR SECRET ORDER. INCLUDE ACTIVITIES, A SECRET MEETING PLACE, RITUALS TO PERFORM, AND SOMETHING TO MAKE AS A GROUP.

NOTE: YOU DO NOT HAVE TO CONDUCT A MEETING IF YOU DON'T WANT TO. SOMETIMES IT IS JUST FUN TO THINK ABOUT WHAT IT WOULD BE LIKE.

DANGER
HIGH VOLTAGE
DO NOT ENTER

SPREAD THE WORD OF THE SECRET ORDER. CREATE A PIECE OF GUERRILLA ART WITH AN IMAGE OF YOUR CHOOSING TO LEAVE IN A PUBLIC PLACE. THIS IMAGE WILL BE YOUR SECRET ORDER SYMBOL. SOME METHODS OF REPRODUCTION YOU CAN USE: DRAWING, STENCILING, RUBBER STAMP (CARVE YOUR OWN OUT OF RUBBER ERASERS), STICKERS, OR POSTERS. MAKE SURE IT IS A NON-PERMANENT MEDIUM (SUCH AS PAPER, CHALK, BIODEGRADABLE GLUE, OR WHEAT PASTE).

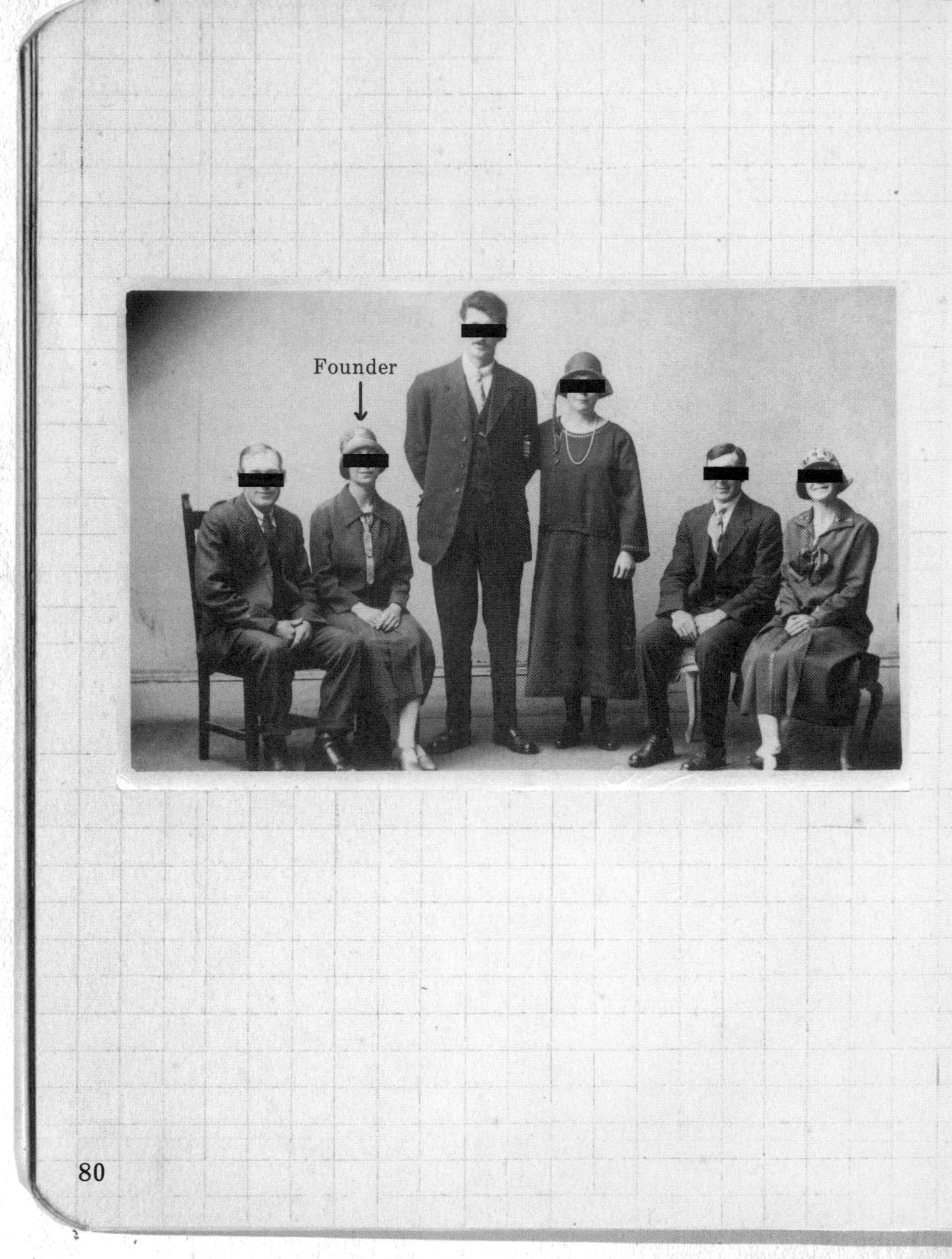
Founder

CREATE YOUR OWN VERSION OF THE HISTORY OF THE SECRET ORDER OF THE LOST FOREST.

REWARD YOURSELF

Don't wait for others to approve of your accomplishments. You are a hard worker who deserves credit! Your talents are wide and varied, so what if some of them aren't recognized by the world yet. It's time you got some recognition. Create your own reward badges for a job well done (using the templates below). You can make them for any activities you wish. Give them to friends! Wear them with pride. Use them in your own secret order. Go ahead. You deserve it!

Ideas for Activities

1. Plant a secret garden. Sprinkle seeds somewhere (choose something the birds will like).
2. Sketch as many different leaves as you can find.
3. Create a Scavenger Hunt for someone else.
4. Have a bird spotting contest.
5. Go on a hunt for the perfect walking stick.
6. Collect flat things to glue into your Secret Book.

Secret Order Badge Templates

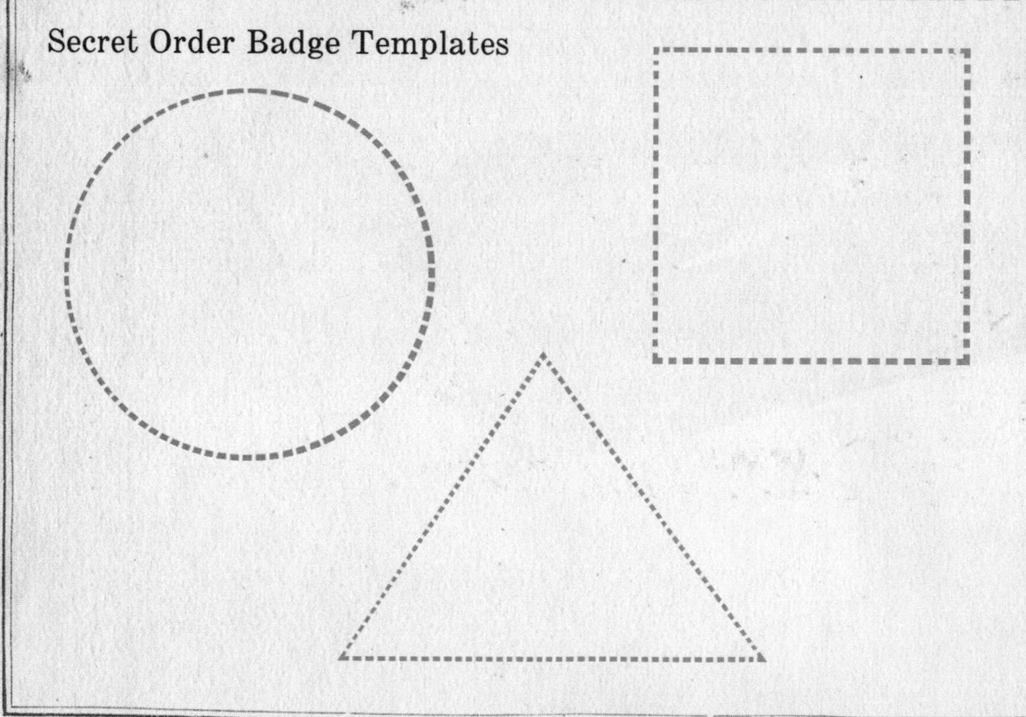

Is modern life getting you down? Do you feel overwhelmed, anxious, and tired a lot of the time? Is technology making you feel distracted, disconnected? Do you find you spend more time in front of screens and less time with friends and family?

Well, we have the answer for you! Join the **Secret Order of the Lost Forest** and you will soon remember what it is like to feel the wind on your face again!

How to Join

1. Turn off the television and computer.
2. Cut out and fill in this form and head outside.
3. Leave the form in the hole of a tree.
4. Follow the manifesto on page 3.

Join now! Lifetime membership is free. This is a limited time offer.

- -

Name: ______________________________

Address: ______________________________

____

INSTRUCTION MANUAL

Lot No.
I1 4WH1 FA
3A AO W
6AGDO1K FA
31F
FA I41D1 I1
WD1

THE LOCK*

* THE KEY IS HIDDEN SOMEWHERE IN THE <u>INSTRUCTION MANUAL</u> WITH A SECRET CODE.

SECRET RESEARCH NOTES

Department of ______________________________

Subject ______________________________

Name ______________________________

Address ______________________________

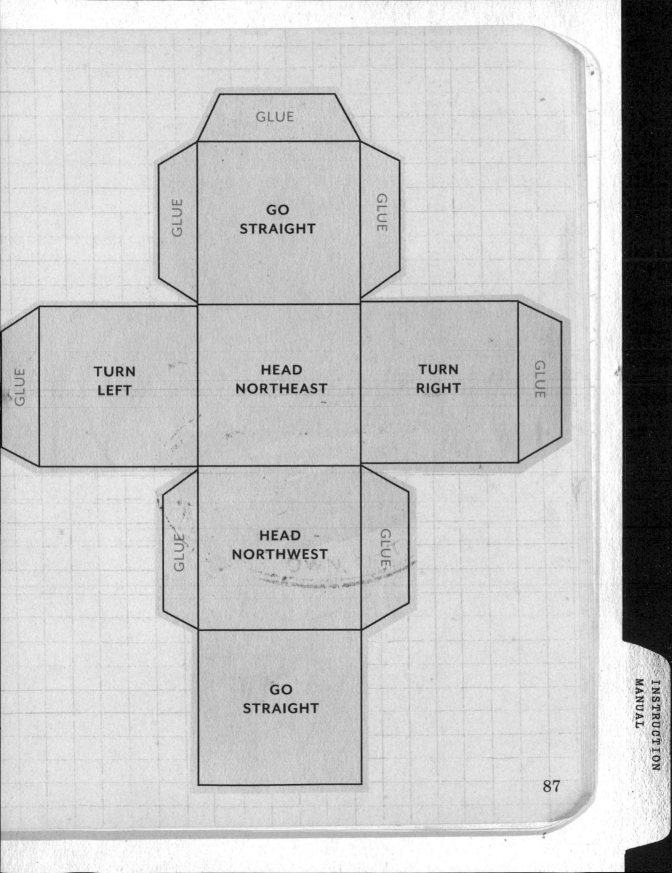

GLUE

GLUE

GO STRAIGHT

GLUE

GLUE

TURN LEFT

HEAD NORTHEAST

TURN RIGHT

GLUE

GLUE

HEAD NORTHWEST

GLUE

GO STRAIGHT

INSTRUCTION
MANUAL

Checklist

- [ ] Manifesto
- [ ] Lock
- [ ] Secret Order
- [ ] Secret Headquarters
- [ ] Map
- [ ] Dice
- [ ] Material Exploration
- [ ] The List
- [ ] Sensory Experiments
- [ ] Collection Device
- [ ] Scavenger Hunt
- [ ] Animal Mascot
- [ ] Guerrilla Art
- [ ] Invitation
- [ ] People Watching
- [ ] Secret Meeting
- [ ] Journaling
- [ ] Imaginary Landmarks
- [ ] Wearable Item
- [ ] Book Passage
- [ ] Imaginary World
- [ ] Hand
- [ ] Famous Explorer
- [ ] The Tree
- [ ] Code Cards
- [ ] Hidden Identity
- [ ] Animal Observation
- [ ] Patterns
- [ ] Paper Trail
- [ ] Leave a Trail
- [ ] Camera Hunting
- [ ] Imaginary Things
- [ ] Buried Treasure
- [ ] Random Experience Generator
- [ ] Clouds
- [ ] Color Map
- [ ] Museum
- [ ] Ad for Secret Order
- [ ] Skymap
- [ ] Repurpose
- [ ] Secret History
- [ ] Page List/Membership Cards

Use this space to write a long list of some kind.

Membership Card #47320

Branch: ____________________________
Name: ______________________________
City/Town, State: ____________________
____
____
Codename: __________________________
Expires: ____________________________
Signature: __________________________
____

Membership Card #47321

Branch: ____________________________
Name: ______________________________
City/Town, State: ____________________
____
____
Codename: __________________________
Expires: ____________________________
Signature: __________________________
____

Membership Card #47322

Branch: ____________________________
Name: ______________________________
City/Town, State: ____________________
____
____
Codename: __________________________
Expires: ____________________________
Signature: __________________________
____

LOST FOREST PUBLISHING CO.
VICTORIA DR 1100
1190

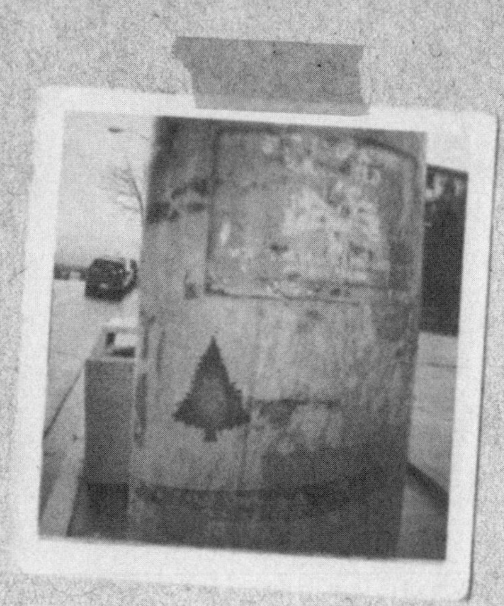

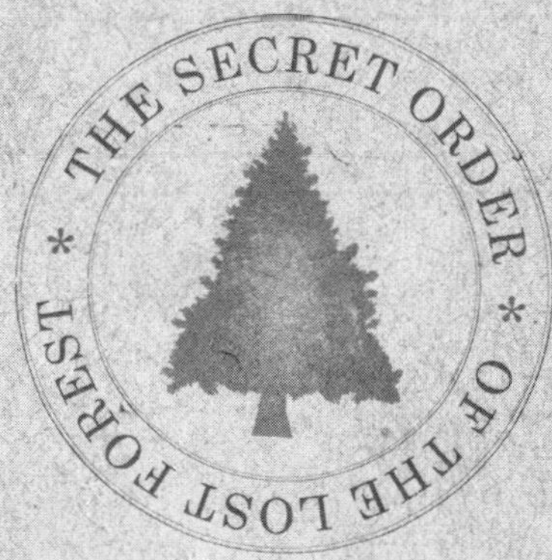
THE SECRET ORDER * OF THE LOST FOREST *

OPERATE IN SECRECY.
CREATE YOUR OWN RULES.
SEEK AND YOU SHALL FIND.
THIS BOOK CANNOT BE DESTROYED.
YOU MUST PASS IT ON.

LOST FOREST PUBLISHISHING CO.

BACK
COVER

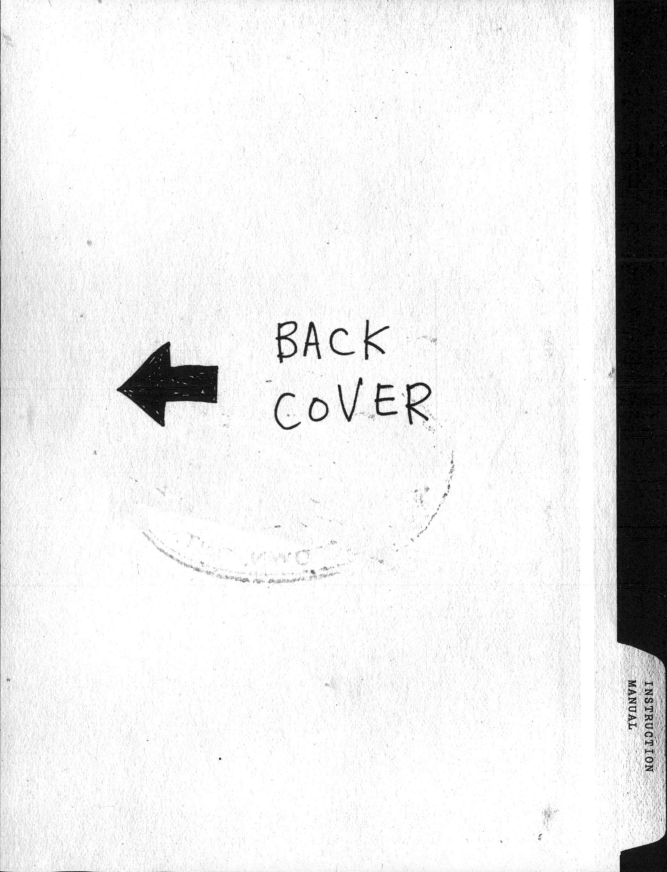

INSTRUCTION
MANUAL

JOURNAL ENTRY

Create a journal entry about completing the Instruction Manual. This entry will be the beginning of your continuation of the mission outside of the confines of this book. Over time you might wish to grow your secret order, create your own explorations, or even create another book entirely. It is up to you.

Date:
Time:
Location:
Notes:

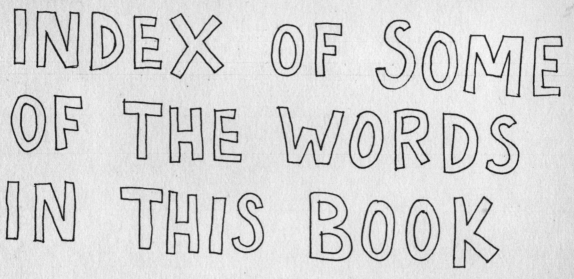

INDEX OF SOME OF THE WORDS IN THIS BOOK

(Fill it in.)

Word	Page name

ABOUT THE AUTHOR

(Fill it in about yourself.)

IMPORTANT: DO NOT READ THE NEXT PAGE UNLESS YOU HAVE COMPLETED THE ENTIRE BOOK.

DEAR READER,

IF YOU HAVE GOTTEN THIS FAR THEN I MUST ASSUME YOU HAVE COMPLETED YOUR OWN VERSION OF THE INSTRUCTION MANUAL. YOU SHOULD FEEL FANTASTIC! PLEASE TREAT YOURSELF TO A REWARD OF SOME KIND.

BUT YOU MAY BE WONDERING ABOUT SOLVING THE MYSTERY. WHAT ABOUT THE CREATOR OF THE INSTRUCTION MANUAL — DOES HE OR SHE EXIST?

THE ANSWER IS **YES**. BECAUSE YOU HAVE BECOME THE CREATOR. YOU AND YOUR EXPERIENCE WITH THIS BOOK ARE NOW THE MAIN FOCUS, THEY CANNOT BE SEPARATED. YOU ARE THE MAIN CHARACTER AND THE AUTHOR. THE PLOT HAS BECOME CONNECTED TO YOUR LIFE. THIS IS YOUR STORY, AND YOUR BOOK.

IT IS ENTIRELY POSSIBLE THAT THE MANUAL I FOUND IS NOT THE ORIGINAL, THAT IT HAS ALREADY BEEN REPRODUCED MANY TIMES. MAYBE THERE IS A LONG TRAIL OF MANUALS THAT SPREADS WELL INTO HISTORY, IN WHICH CASE TRACKING THE ORIGINAL AUTHOR WOULD BE NEARLY IMPOSSIBLE.

YOU MAY ALSO BE WONDERING WHY I CHOSE TO PASS THIS TASK ON TO YOU. I SUPPOSE THAT IS THE ANSWER TO THE MYSTERY AS WELL... WHOEVER CREATED THE ORIGINAL INSTRUCTION MANUAL LEFT IT OUT IN THE WORLD TO BE FOUND, SO THAT WE COULD CREATE SOMETHING IN OUR OWN UNIQUE VOICE. IT SEEMED IMPORTANT TO ME TO MAKE THE MISSION AVAILABLE TO OTHERS WHO WERE DRAWN TO IT AS WELL. NOW YOU ARE BEING ASKED TO FIND A WAY TO REPRODUCE YOUR VERSION OF THE BOOK, LIKE A KIND OF ZINE. PUT IT OUT INTO THE WORLD FOR SOMEONE ELSE TO FIND AND FOLLOW (RESEARCH: MEME). YOU MAY INCLUDE YOUR OWN INSTRUCTIONS WITH IT IF YOU'D LIKE. IN THIS WAY "THE MANUAL" WILL REMAIN IN EXISTENCE FOR YEARS TO COME.

BECAUSE, IN THE END, ISN'T THAT WHY WE ARE ALL HERE... TO CREATE SOMETHING IN OUR OWN UNIQUE VOICE AND SHARE IT WITH OTHERS?

WITH MUCH AFFECTION,

KERI SMITH

SOME BOOKS

the author found useful while working with the Instruction Manual.

Trees of North America: A Guide to Field Identification, Revised and Updated (Golden Field Guides Series), by C. Frank Brockman and Rebecca Marrilees (St. Martin's, 2001)

Tom Brown's Field Guide to Living with the Earth, by Tom Brown Jr. (Berkley, 1986)

Coyote's Guide to Connecting with Nature, by Jon Young, Ellen Haas, Evan McGown (Owlink Media, 2010)

Mountaineering Essays, by John Muir (University of Utah Press, 1997)

Tracking and Trailing: The Good Spy Guide, by Ruth Thompson, Judy Hindley (Edc Pub, 1978)

The Norton Book of Nature Writing, John Elder (Editor), Robert Finch (Editor) (W.W. Norton & Co., 2002)

Other sources of inspiration:

Edward Abbey
Opal Whiteley
Emily Carr
Annie Dillard
Wendell Barry
Rick Bass
Rachel Carson
Gary Snider
Bill McKibben
E.O. Wilson

Template

Template

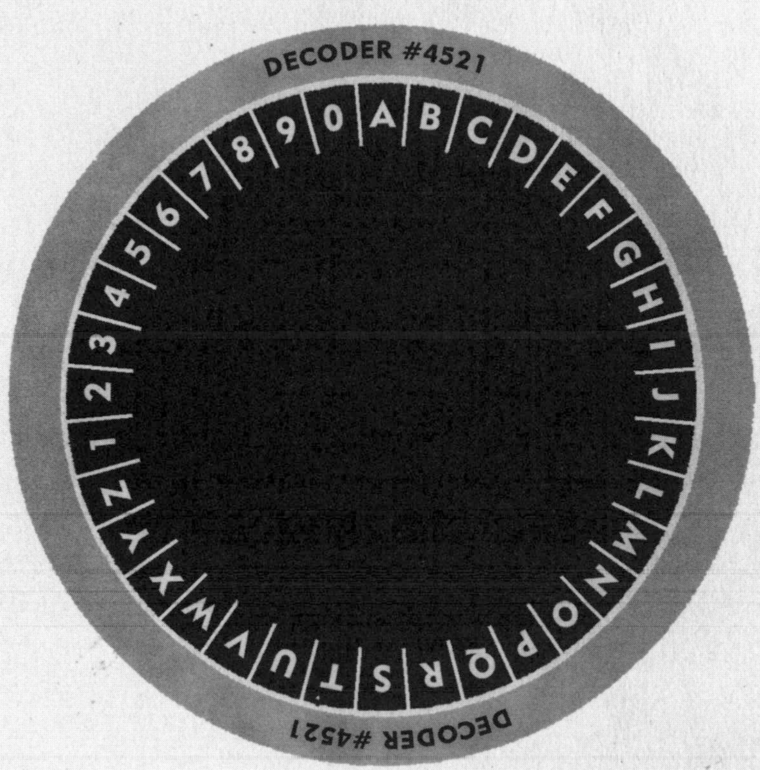
DECODER #4521
0 A B C D E F G H I J K L M N O P Q R S T U V W X Y Z 1 2 3 4 5 6 7 8 9
DECODER #4521

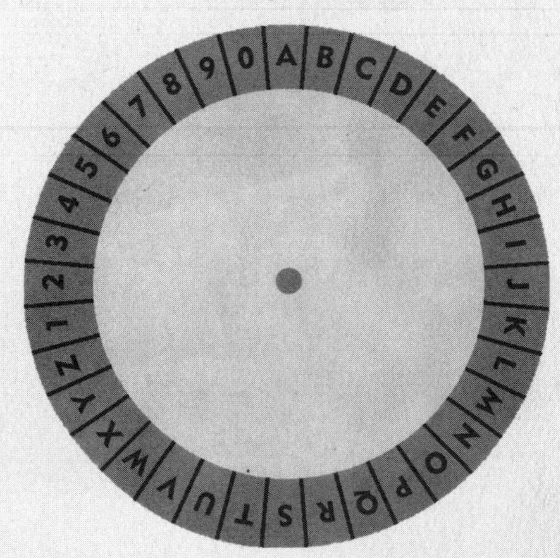
0 A B C D E F G H I J K L M N O P Q R S T U V W X Y Z 1 2 3 4 5 6 7 8 9

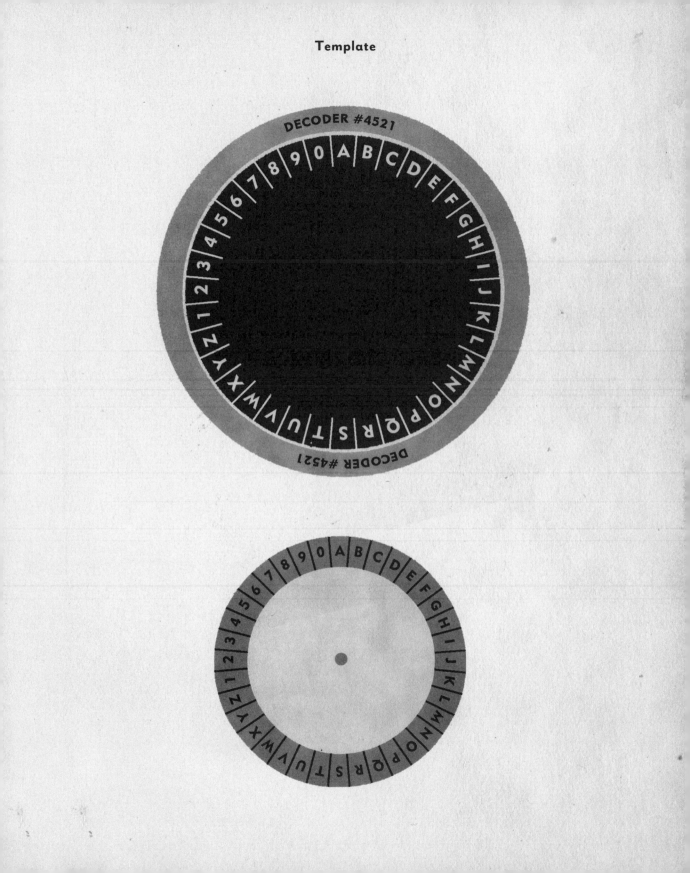